D0330965

Your word is a lamp to my feet and a light to my path.

PSALM 119:105 NKJV

THE 150
MOST IMPORTANT
BIBLE VERSES

Presented to:

_____

Presented by:

_____

Date:

_____

Test all things;
hold fast what is good.

1 Thessalonians 5:21 NKJV

THE 150
MOST IMPORTANT
BIBLE VERSES

THOMAS NELSON
Since 1798

NASHVILLE   DALLAS   MEXICO CITY   RIO DE JANEIRO   BEIJING

The 150 Most Important Bible Verses © 2007 by GRQ, Inc. Brentwood, Tennessee 37027

This book was compiled from the following books in *The 100 Most Important Bible Verses* series:

The 100 Most Important Bible Verses © 2005 by GRQ, Inc. Manuscript: Vicki J. Kuyper

The 100 Most Important Bible Verses for Men © 2006 by GRQ, Inc. Manuscript: Robin Schmitt

The 100 Most Important Bible Verses for Women © 2005 by GRQ, Inc. Manuscript: Jeanette & Mark Littleton

The 100 Most Important Bible Verses for Teens © 2005 by GRQ, Inc. Manuscript: Robi Lipscomb & J. Heyward Rogers

The 100 Most Important Bible Verses for Leaders © 2006 by GRQ, Inc. Manuscript: Sheila Cornea

All rights reserved. No portion of this book may be reproduced, stored in a retrieval system, or transmitted in any form or by any means—electronic, mechanical, photocopy, recording, scanning, or other—except for brief quotations in critical reviews or articles, without the prior written permission of the publisher.

Published in Nashville, Tennessee, by Thomas Nelson. Thomas Nelson is a registered trademark of Thomas Nelson, Inc.

Thomas Nelson, Inc. titles may be purchased in bulk for educational, business, fund-raising, or sales promotional use. For information, please e-mail SpecialMarkets@ThomasNelson.com.

Scripture quotations are from the following sources:

THE CONTEMPORARY ENGLISH VERSION (CEV). © 1991 by the American Bible Society. Used by permission.

THE GOOD NEWS TRANSLATION (GNT). © 1976, 1992 by The American Bible Society. Used by permission. All rights reserved.

The Message by Eugene H. Peterson (MSG). © 1993, 1994, 1995, 1996, 2000. Used by permission of NavPress Publishing Group. All rights reserved.

NEW AMERICAN STANDARD BIBLE® (NASB). © The Lockman Foundation 1960, 1962, 1963, 1968, 1971, 1972, 1973, 1975, 1977, 1995. Used by permission.

NEW CENTURY VERSION® (NCV). © 2005 by Thomas Nelson, Inc. Used by permission. All rights reserved.

THE NEW KING JAMES VERSION (NKJV). © 1982 by Thomas Nelson, Inc. Used by permission. All rights reserved.

HOLY BIBLE: NEW LIVING TRANSLATION (NLT). © 1996. Used by permission of Tyndale House Publishers, Inc., Wheaton, Illinois 60189. All rights reserved.

The Living Bible (TLB). © 1971. Used by permission of Tyndale House Publishers, Inc., Wheaton, Illinois 60189. All rights reserved.

Design: Thatcher Design, Nashville, Tennessee

ISBN: 978-1-4041-1375-6

Printed in China

10 11 12 RRD 5 4 3

Contents

Important Bible Verses for Everyone

Important Bible Verses for Men

Important Bible Verses for Women

Important Bible Verses for Teens

Important Bible Verses for Leaders

Introduction

Reading the Bible from cover to cover can seem like a daunting task. After all, the Bible is a big book that doesn't read like an ordinary book. That's because the Bible is anything but ordinary. It's a love letter from God to the world. Instead of having a beginning, a middle, and an end, the Bible tells an ongoing story, one in which you play an important part.

The 150 Most Important Bible Verses is designed to help you get better acquainted with God and his words one step at a time. Each brief chapter focuses on a bite-size portion of the Bible. You can discover more about the cultural, historical, and scriptural context of the verse, as well as gain insight into the verse's underlying theme and life-changing truth. You will also find ideas on how to apply what you learn to how you live.

No verse in the Bible can stand alone without the support of every word God has provided. However, by reading *The 150 Most Important Bible Verses*, you'll get an overview of what the Bible has to say. It will help you better know where to turn when you need to hear what God says about a specific topic, such as contentment, love, problems, or peace. May *The 150 Most Important Bible Verses* help you know more about the Bible and its author in a deeper and more relevant way.

⤳⑂∅

IMPORTANT
BIBLE VERSES
FOR EVERYONE

God's word is alive and working and is sharper than a double-edged sword. It cuts all the way into us, where the soul and the spirit are joined, to the center of our joints and bones. And it judges the thoughts and feelings in our hearts.

HEBREWS 4:12 NCV

Jesus said, "Your Father knows the things you need before you ask him."

Matthew 6:8 NCV

Father Knows Best

Jesus gave his disciples the Lord's Prayer as an example of how to pray. Right before he spoke those famous words, Jesus shared a few reasons *why* one should pray. To do this, he provided two examples—negative ones. Jesus said the Pharisees prayed in public because they wanted to be seen as holy by other people. He also said idol worshipers prayed, repeating themselves over and over, because they believed that the more frequently they asked for something, the better chance they had of having their request granted. After those negative examples, Jesus spoke the reassurance that God already knows what you need.

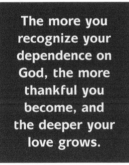

At first, his words may seem to provide a reason why *not* to pray, instead of why to pray. If God knows what you need before you ask, why bother asking in the first place? Jesus' point is, the purpose of prayer isn't to be noticed by other people—or even by God. God already notices you. He knows everything about you and your life. Prayer is not a way to draw God's attention to your needs. It is a way to draw your attention to how much you need God.

Your greatest continual need is to better know and love God. Communicating with him about the details of your life keeps you aware of how involved he already is. It also helps you see how many of your needs

> **The more you recognize your dependence on God, the more thankful you become, and the deeper your love grows.**

he fills every day. The more you recognize your dependence on God, the more thankful you become, and the deeper your love grows.

The Lord's Prayer teaches you to pray for your daily bread. Jesus' words from Matthew don't contradict that lesson. They're a reminder that God needs to be involved in your life, not merely informed about it.

If we confess our sins, He is faithful and just to forgive us our sins and to cleanse us from all unrighteousness.

1 JOHN 1:9 NKJV

Fully Forgiven

Being a scapegoat is not a job most people would volunteer for. After all, it implies taking the blame for what others have done. But in the Old Testament, God offered forgiveness to his people in exactly this way. The priest would lay his hands on the head of a goat and symbolically transfer onto the scapegoat the blame for the sins the people had committed. The priest then sent the animal into the wilderness to take the people's offenses far away. Once the scapegoat removed the people's sins, God in his holiness could once again draw near to the people he loved.

In the New Testament, a different kind of scapegoat appeared—Jesus Christ. As God's Son, he willingly chose to bear the offenses of the whole world, to take the blame for everything the people had done against God since the dawn of time and until the end of it. Jesus was innocent of the sins and transgresions of the people, and yet, as the scapegoat, he took the punishment for them all so that his beloved people could be spared.

The great hope and promise of this verse is that it tells you exactly what you need to do to allow Jesus to be your scapegoat, which opens the door to God's forgiveness in your life. *To confess* simply means "to agree." Take a few moments each day to agree with God about how well your thoughts,

Move forward with confidence, fully forgiven and free from guilt.

words, and actions have lined up with what he desires for your life. Move forward with confidence, fully forgiven and free from guilt.

Once God forgives you, all traces of your past offenses are gone. His forgiveness wipes away any feelings of guilt or blame.

Jesus said, "I leave you peace; my peace I give you. I do not give it to you as the world does. So don't let your hearts be troubled or afraid."

JOHN 14:27 NCV

Jesus' Legacy of Peace

In the Jewish culture, the Hebrew word *shalom* is a customary greeting for both "hello" and "good-bye." *Shalom* means "peace" and so much more. It implies a wish for health, prosperity, and wholeness, as well as a wish for an absence of both internal and external strife.

As Jesus prepared to say good-bye to his closest friends on the night of the Last Supper, he bid them shalom. Jesus' words of farewell were far more than a traditional blessing.

They were a gift only the Prince of Peace himself could offer. Jesus offered his followers peace of mind and heart, a peace unlike that of the world they knew, which depended on favorable circumstances. Jesus' offer of peace depended solely on his followers' relationship with him.

These words of Jesus are like his Last Will and Testament. In the same way that a will records how to divide possessions among the survivors of the one who died, John 14:27 is a record of your inheritance. Jesus bequeathed a priceless treasure to all those who follow him, including you. In fact, his gift has set you up for life—both this one and the next. That's because the wholeness found in

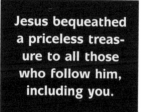

Jesus bequeathed a priceless treasure to all those who follow him, including you.

Jesus' gift of peace is at the heart of true happiness. As you pursue peace by pursuing Jesus, you'll find you are holding the true key to living the good life.

Jesus' gift of peace offers you an alternative to fear and worry, a foretaste of heaven available here and now. As with any inheritance, you have to accept it and use it to enjoy its true benefits.

Though the LORD is supreme, he takes care of those who are humble, but he stays away from the proud.

PSALM 138:6 NCV

The Peril of Pride

In the ancient Middle East, there were many myths about powerful monsters and primeval sea creatures. One Canaanite legend told of a sea monster named Rahab who fought against God's creation of the universe. The word *rahab* is Hebrew for both "acting stormily" and "arrogance." In the same way that the sea creature refused to believe God's power could be greater than its own, arrogant people believe they can succeed in life solely by their own strength.

The bases for human pride are as much a myth as that

sea creature. Physical abilities, IQ, talents, and accomplishments are all God's gifts. You can add effort to what God has given you, but the basic building blocks are all courtesy of him.

Basing your life on a myth is bad enough. However, the most destructive thing about pride is that it acts like a God-repellent and pushes God away from the center of your life. As God keeps his distance from the proud, his gifts of guidance, wisdom, and comfort

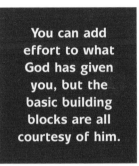

You can add effort to what God has given you, but the basic building blocks are all courtesy of him.

move out of reach. While God notices pride right away, you may be unaware of its presence. Ask a close friend if he or she sees evidence of pride in your life. Ask God to help you become more aware of your true motives, and then battle pride with the truth of who God is. The more you come to know and understand him, the more accurate a picture you'll have of yourself—and the more humility will replace pride in your life.

Whenever you feel pride raise its arrogant head in your life, picture the sea monster, Rahab, battling—and losing to— God's supremacy.

I will give you a new heart and put a new spirit within you; I will take the heart of stone out of your flesh and give you a heart of flesh.

EZEKIEL 36:26 NKJV

Heart Transplant

A beating heart is a sign of life. Physically, your heart beats regularly. But spiritually, until you get to know God firsthand, your heart is flat-lining. God promised the prophet Ezekiel (along with everyone who chooses to follow God) the ultimate heart transplant—replacing stone with flesh. This "flesh" is humanity as God originally created it, which is more than simply being human. It is the promise of being fully alive—physically, emotionally, and spiritually—in both this life and the next.

The people of Israel believed a person's "heart" reveals who a person really is. The heart cannot put on airs or be something it is not. It is the emotional and spiritual center of every individual. When God's Spirit becomes the center of people's lives, the Bible says that they are "born again." Along with a new heart comes a new start.

However, this heart transplant is possible only through the power of God's Spirit. Trying to become more loving, generous, and kind through self-effort can never bring a heart of stone to life. Only God's gift of his presence can jump-start a heart into permanent change. God's Spirit at work in you enables you to hear God's voice as he guides your decisions, to see his hand

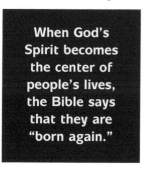

When God's Spirit becomes the center of people's lives, the Bible says that they are "born again."

as he moves through circumstances, and to fulfill his plans for you to become the person he created you to be.

Through God's words to Ezekiel, you are given a beautiful metaphor to help you understand what happens when God's Spirit comes into your life: you are fully alive for the very first time.

What we have is one body with many parts, each its proper size and in its proper place. No part is important on its own.

1 Corinthians 12:20 msg

Joint Venture

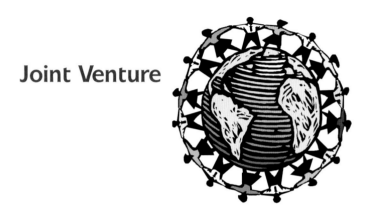

Your body is the perfect picture of how God designed community to work. Every part is interdependent and is vital to the health and strength of the other parts. If your lungs took the day off, your brain would cease to function. If your muscles went on strike, your feet wouldn't be able get you out of bed and off to work.

Paul's picture of the cooperative human body illustrates how every individual is vital to the health of God's church as a whole. It also demonstrates how every part is signifi-

cant. One part isn't more important than another. You should
not regard the person who preaches
on Sunday morning as more important than the one who cleans the
building before the service. Each individual is necessary. Every gift God

> **Every gift God gives has a purpose and a place to help fulfill his perfect plan.**

gives has a purpose and a place to help fulfill his perfect plan.

People often encounter two pitfalls when they evaluate
their significance by comparing their gifts with others':
(1) they believe their gifts are too small or too big, or (2) they
feel that what they do really doesn't matter or that everything
would fall apart without them. Paul's words in 1 Corinthians
guide you toward the true measure of significance. Though
you are of eternal significance to God, your significance on
this earth comes solely from what you are a part of—God's
body here on earth.

—⁕—

Understanding your significance, and the significance of others, will help you keep a humble, realistic view of yourself. It
will also enable you to work more harmoniously in community with others.

All have sinned; all fall short of God's glorious standard. Yet now God in his gracious kindness declares us not guilty. He has done this through Christ Jesus, who has freed us by taking away our sins.

ROMANS 3:23–24 NLT

Missing the Mark

When a person competes in the pole vault, he is focused on doing one thing—jumping higher than the mark where the pole's been set. Once he has jumped, there can be only two outcomes. He either cleared the mark or fell short. If he failed in his attempt to clear the pole, whether he missed by an inch or a foot doesn't matter. He still failed.

The same is true with sin. The Hebrew word for *sin* literally means "to miss the mark." Everyone sins by choosing to go his own way instead of God's way. Some people miss God's mark by an inch; others miss by a mile. How close you come doesn't matter. Close isn't close enough. The moral pole God has

The good news is that this perfect and faultless God is also perfect and loving.

set for you to clear is a high one; it is so high that it's impossible to continually clear it on your own. A perfect, holy God can't embrace anything less than perfect. The good news is that this perfect and faultless God is also perfect and loving. That's why he provided a way for you to clear the bar more consistently, as well as a means for you to avoid a penalty when you miss the mark.

It is important to recognize that everyone sins. Shift your focus to the future, not to the past. Because of Jesus, guilt and the fear of punishment no longer weigh you down. You are free to jump higher than ever before.

When you miss the mark, ask for God's forgiveness, learn from your mistake, and keep moving forward.

I'm eager to encourage you in your faith, but I also want to be encouraged by yours. In this way, each of us will be a blessing to the other.

ROMANS 1:12 NLT

Sharing Your Strength

God is not the only One with the power to bless. You, too, can build others up by showing them special favor, which is what a blessing really is. One way is through the gift of encouragement. Paul expressed his desire to share this valuable gift with other believers who lived in Rome. He'd never met them, and neither had any of the other apostles. But that didn't stop Paul from longing to comfort and strengthen others who shared his faith in God.

Paul's words are a practical example of God's love at work. Love cannot exist in a vacuum. You have to share it.

When you encourage others by your loving example, actions, words, or prayers, you'll discover that your gift comes with a bonus. You will, in turn,

> **Love cannot exist in a vacuum. You have to share it.**

be encouraged. In the Greek language, *to encourage* means "to share your strength with others" as well as "to be mutually comforted." The more you take the opportunity to cheer on and support those around you, the more you'll experience the joy that love can bring.

God has used Paul's words and the example of his life to strengthen and inspire people for more than two thousand years. You never know when a simple word of encouragement to a friend or even a stranger will cause a ripple effect that will be felt throughout eternity. Put the principle behind Paul's words to the test today. God can turn your simple gift of encouragement into a tremendous blessing.

Be encouraged, and act on what you've learned. Strengthen others by sharing how much they mean to you and to God.

The Word became a human and lived among us. We saw his glory—the glory that belongs to the only Son of the Father—and he was full of grace and truth.

JOHN 1:14 NCV

Special Delivery

The day God came to earth is much more than a sweet tale on which to base a holiday. It is a miracle of dynamic proportions, and John tells the wonder of it all. God himself came to live on earth. That is the heart of the Christmas story. The God of the universe made his home here on earth so that people could better understand him, connect with him, and experience his kindness. The Word is God's most intimate, and informative, communication with those whom he created.

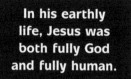

It is interesting that such a pivotal verse about Jesus does not even contain his name. That's because *Word* was a powerful symbol in both Greek philosophy and Jewish tradition. The Greeks referred to *logos* or *Word* as the creative force that brought the world

> **In his earthly life, Jesus was both fully God and fully human.**

into being. Everyone at that time understood that referring to Jesus as the Word was the same as calling him the eternal Creator.

If you're going to believe in this eternal Creator, you need to understand who he is. The biggest mistake people make about Jesus is to minimize either his deity or his humanity. In his earthly life, Jesus was both fully God and fully human. John emphasized this point throughout his entire Gospel. Although both the Old and New Testaments are filled with important verses about Jesus, John 1:14 clearly states who Jesus is and what he wants to impart to you.

Jesus' humanity enabled him to relate to your human problems, while his divinity gave him the power to help you overcome them.

Jesus said, "The thief does not come except to steal, and to kill, and to destroy. I have come that they may have life, and that they may have it more abundantly."

JOHN 10:10 NKJV

Living Life to the Fullest

Jesus often used parables and metaphors to help people get a better picture of the principles and truths he was talking about. He referred to himself as things like a vine, a lamb, or a bridegroom. He also described himself as the Good Shepherd. He wanted his followers to understand the difference between how a good shepherd cares and sacrifices for the benefit of his sheep, while thieves and hired hands use sheep only to benefit themselves. Jesus wanted them to know he was a leader who always had his followers' best interests at heart.

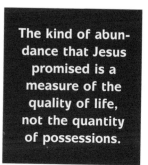

Jesus proclaimed the end result of this tender care for his sheep, which makes the verse one of the most important verses in the Bible. It is Jesus' statement of purpose; it is his promise to those who follow him. That includes you. What Jesus promised is life. Not just ordinary, breathing-in-and-out, making-it-by-the-seat-of-your-pants life, but an authentic, eternal, hang-on-to-your-seats-because-another-miracle's-coming abundant life.

> The kind of abundance that Jesus promised is a measure of the quality of life, not the quantity of possessions.

The kind of abundance that Jesus promised is a measure of the quality of life, not the quantity of possessions. You can't measure this abundance in square footage or bottom lines. Jesus promised to provide a surplus of what makes life worth living—things like love, grace, guidance, forgiveness, and joy. These are Jesus' gifts to you, a life that is overflowing with riches of the heart that no one can ever take away.

Keeping in mind Jesus' promise to you of an abundant life gives you reason for constant hope and thanks. It also fosters contentment by helping you find joy in the abundance of what matters most.

God is our refuge and strength, a very present help in trouble. Therefore we will not fear, even though the earth be removed, and though the mountains be carried into the midst of the sea . . . "Be still, and know that I am God."

PSALM 46:1–2, 10 NKJV

Stop, Look, Listen, and Trust

The Psalms are a tapestry of human emotions. The poetry of prayer weaves together anger, fear, joy, longing, despair, praise, and passion. These verses sum up God's response to those prayers. Their truth is the thread of peace and comfort that runs through the entire book of Psalms, as well as the rest of the Bible — and the life of every individual who walks with God. God's answer to those who are emotionally troubled is brief and straightforward: stop and remember who is on your side.

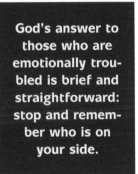

Psalm 46 talks about earthquakes felling mountains, cities being destroyed, nations being in an uproar, kingdoms crumbling. It talks about the final destruction of the world itself. The overall tone of the psalm is anything but quiet and still. One sentence, however, says to "be still," and the focal point of emotion changes from outside chaos to internal rest.

That's why this psalm was written as a song. It proclaimed a message everyone needed to hear.

God's answer to those who are emotionally troubled is brief and straightforward: stop and remember who is on your side.

Let the truth of these verses find a home in your heart today. When life gets busy or chaotic, it's easy to get distracted. You wind up focusing on problems instead of the One who holds the answer to your problems in his hands. When that happens, stop. Focus on who God is and how much he loves you. Share your own heartfelt psalm of prayer with the God of power and compassion. Be still and know God is near.

The words in Psalm 46 hold incredible power when it comes to knowing God is near in any and every situation. Memorize them. Meditate on them. Keep them close at heart for when you need them most.

In all the work you are doing, work the best you can. Work as if you were doing it for the Lord, not for people.

COLOSSIANS 3:23 NCV

Job Description: Excellence

Work is a noble calling. God commends people for doing it well, and he also does work himself. When God created the world, he worked. The excellence of his work is evident in everything he made. He even took a day off to review the results of his efforts and declared them "good." God continues to work, sustaining what he created that very first week in the world's history.

Since God created you in his image, work should be a part of your life. Doing it well reflects God's creativity and character. It is easy, however, to lose your motivation when a job is difficult or you become bored with doing the same thing day after day. Paul's words to the Colossians can help you keep your work in its proper perspective. Working the best you can literally means working "out from the soul." You are not working simply to pay the bills, please your boss, or pass the time of day. God set this job in front of you. When you do your job well, God notices, even if no one else does.

Working the best you can literally means working "out from the soul."

This section of Colossians was originally directed toward slaves. It encouraged them to remain positive and productive, even if they were working in bondage under a tyrant. If a slave, who could be beaten even if he did a job well, could strive for excellence by maintaining a Colossians 3:23 perspective, certainly it is something you can do in whatever job is facing you.

Focus on God's perspective throughout the day and imagine at all times that he is your boss.

May God himself, the God who makes everything holy and whole, make you holy and whole, put you together—spirit, soul, and body—and keep you fit for the coming of our Master, Jesus Christ.

1 THESSALONIANS 5:23 MSG

Piecing Life Together

A jigsaw puzzle is made up of multiple parts. It is only when these parts are put together, when the puzzle is whole and complete, that you see the picture it was designed to display. Your life is the same way. Your life is made up of many complex components: family life, job, hobbies, physical health, emotional state, present circumstances, past experiences, hopes for the future, relationship with God. It would be easy to feel that your life is fragmented, like unconnected pieces of a puzzle that don't seem to fit. But that isn't the way you were designed.

God designed you to be whole and complete, where every part of your life interconnects with his love and his plan. This doesn't happen automatically or overnight. That is why the apostle Paul asked God to help the people in the church at Thessalonica to continue to move closer toward wholeness in their lives.

> **God designed you to be whole and complete, where every part of your life interconnects with his love and his plan.**

He recognized that people cannot achieve the process of maturity that leads to wholeness through self-effort. It requires the power of God. Paul's prayer is one you need to pray for yourself.

Ask God to help pull the pieces of your life together according to his original design. As you choose to keep God at the center of your life, you'll find your own unique "picture" becoming more complete. Your job, your relationships, and your dreams work together, linked to one another because they are each solidly linked back to God.

~∞

Let Paul's prayer make you more aware of the big picture behind what's going on in your life. Ask God to help you get a better glimpse of what that really is.

See how the farmer waits for the precious fruit of the earth, waiting patiently for it until it receives the early and latter rain. You also be patient. Establish your hearts, for the coming of the Lord is at hand.

JAMES 5:7–8 NKJV

Watching and Waiting

God's timing is always perfect. He parted the Red Sea when his people needed it most—when they were trapped between the rushing waters and an approaching army. God allowed the water to flow again, but only after Moses and the Israelites had made it safely across. God provided what the people needed at the precise moment that it would make the greatest difference.

From a human vantage point, it isn't always easy to recognize that opportune moment. Waiting for God's answer, when your own internal timer has already gone off, can make you feel as if God isn't listening or he simply doesn't care.

When you find yourself in that situation, take a lesson from this important verse in James and put yourself in a farmer's shoes. You can't rush a perfect harvest or an answer to prayer. As

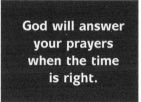

God will answer your prayers when the time is right.

a farmer waits for the fruit of his labor, he doesn't just sit around complaining about how long the growing season is. He continues to work. He trusts God, and his patience grows right along with his fruit.

James provides a valuable tip for those who wait. He advises you to *establish* your heart, which means "to firmly plant your life and expectations in the fertile soil of God's truth." There is a bountiful harvest as certain as the fulfillment of God's promises: the Lord will return; the hard times you face will end; and God will answer your prayers when the time is right.

The image of a patient farmer is an encouraging visual picture for prayer. Picture every prayer as a seed planted in God's will. As you wait, picture them ripening, trusting in God's perfect harvesttime.

You should know that your body is a temple for the Holy Spirit who is in you. You have received the Holy Spirit from God. So you do not belong to yourselves, because you were bought by God for a price. So honor God with your bodies.

1 CORINTHIANS 6:19–20 NCV

God's Dwelling Place

In Paul's day, the city of Corinth was infamous for sexual debauchery and decadence. There was even a slang Greek verb that meant "to act like a Corinthian," which implied that one took part in sexual immorality. The church of Corinth, though filled with true believers in Jesus, continued to struggle with the sinful excesses of its culture. In response to the church's repeated failure to set itself apart for God instead of blending into Corinthian society, Paul directed his comments in a letter to this struggling church. His words today, as well as then, are a good heart-and-body check for every believer.

Thanks to Jesus' sacrifice, your body is now God's home. In the Old Testament, God's presence stayed physically close to his people by dwelling in an elaborate temple complex. God dictated every detail of the temple's construction, as well as strict rules on how to keep it holy and fit for his use. God's Spirit dwelled in an especially sacred part of the temple called the Holy of Holies. In Greek,

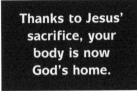

Thanks to Jesus' sacrifice, your body is now God's home.

this place was called *naos*. Paul used that same word here. Your body is God's Holy of Holies.

When a guest comes to your home, you honor that guest by putting things in order and doing all you can to make that person feel comfortable. By taking care of yourself physically and steering clear of sexual sin, you are doing the same for God. You are giving your heavenly Father a warm welcome home.

Your body is a sacred place where God's Spirit dwells. How you treat yourself physically is a reflection of the kind of dwelling place you desire to offer the Father, who loves you.

Do not worry about anything, but pray and ask God for everything you need, always giving thanks. And God's peace, which is so great we cannot understand it, will keep your hearts and minds in Christ Jesus.

PHILIPPIANS 4:6–7 NCV

Panic Attack

Worry is a stealthy, yet formidable, enemy. Worry can creep into your life quietly, masquerading as an acceptable human response to living in an imperfect world. But worry is neither acceptable nor harmless. Worry is a dangerous diversion that leads you to focus on your problems instead of on God, who loves you and is in control. There is an easy, effective way to eliminate worry—pray.

Praying about both the big and small things in your life is a way of constantly realigning your point of view with

 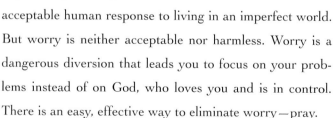

God's perspective. Prayer is more than simply asking God for help. It is also a time of worship and thanks. Thanking God for his past help and blessings is a gift to yourself, as well as to God. Every thank-you serves as a personal reminder of God's love and faithfulness in your life, and it provides you

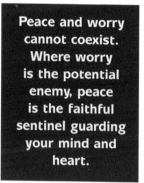

Peace and worry cannot coexist. Where worry is the potential enemy, peace is the faithful sentinel guarding your mind and heart.

with a source of comfort, strength, encouragement, and peace.

Peace and worry cannot coexist. Where worry is the potential enemy, peace is the faithful sentinel guarding your mind and heart. There is nothing passive about the word *guard*. It's a Greek military term that paints a picture of a stronghold being protected by a vigilant garrison of watchmen. When you allow prayer to defeat worry in your life, God's peace will be your watchman through any and every situation.

At the first sign of worry, practice the life-changing principle found in Philippians 4:6–7. Tell God what you're anxious about. Thank him for who he is, for what he has done, and for the peace he provides.

Jesus said, "Come to Me, all you who labor and are heavy laden, and I will give you rest. Take My yoke upon you and learn from Me, for I am gentle and lowly in heart, and you will find rest for your souls."

MATTHEW 11:28–29 NKJV

Sharing the Load

When Jesus spoke to people, he often used parables and word pictures that incorporated familiar everyday situations so his listeners could better identify with the spiritual principles he wanted to share. Jesus spoke about finding rest through being "yoked" to him.

In Jesus' day, a yoke had two distinct meanings. The first was the wooden harness used to link oxen together to plow a field. The second was a slang term referring to Jewish laws and traditions. It was said that Jews were "yoked" to the Torah. In other words, they were burdened by carrying around the Old Testament commands as well

as the numerous additional laws dictated by the Pharisees. Trying to follow that many rules would be exhausting for anyone. Jesus let it be known that relationship, not rule-following, is the key to obedience. Walking closely with God through prayer and allowing his Spirit and his Word to guide you take you from the burden of legalism to the freedom of a righteous life.

> **The rest Jesus offers is a quiet strength and companionship that helps you continue moving forward without burning out physically, mentally, or emotionally.**

The rest Jesus offers isn't an escape from work and struggle. The rest Jesus offers is a quiet strength and companionship that helps you continue moving forward without burning out physically, mentally, or emotionally. All you need to do is "come," "take," and "learn." Learning how to rest in God when times are hard is a process, but walking side by side with the world's greatest Teacher sharing your load is a journey that leads to joy.

When times are difficult, picture Jesus walking alongside you as a reminder that you're not alone. Speak to him honestly about the help you need and your thankfulness for the help he has already provided.

$\mathbf{B}$lessed be the God and Father of our Lord Jesus Christ, the Father of mercies and God of all comfort, who comforts us in all our tribulation, that we may be able to comfort those who are in any trouble, with the comfort with which we ourselves are comforted by God.

2 CORINTHIANS 1:3–4 NKJV

Consolation Prize

The apostle Paul began his second letter to the church in Corinth just as he did his other letters, with a brief introduction that leads straight into thanksgiving. Paul's cause for thanks, however, sets this letter apart. You can be thankful for comfort only if you've known the pain of suffering. Paul certainly did, and so did his Corinthian audience. So does every individual who reads these words today.

Though levels of personal suffering differ, pain and heartache are universal. Yet amid that sobering truth, Paul gave reason for praise. God's comfort is at hand in every type of trouble. The original meaning of the old-fashioned-sounding word *tribulation* covers a lot of ground. It can mean "distress," "affliction," "persecution," or simply "great misery." God's comfort fits any and every situation perfectly.

Through Paul, God provided even more good news: there is a positive, productive side to suffering. As God comforts you, you learn how to better comfort others. This is different from simply being sympathetic toward people and their problems. The Greek word for *comfort* implies action. It means "to come alongside and help." God actively comes alongside you with strength, encouragement, hope, and healing, and you gain the ability to

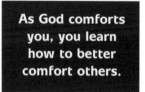

As God comforts you, you learn how to better comfort others.

do the same for others. When you are struggling with difficulty in your life, remember to reach out to God and then to others. God provides comfort to help you become a comforter like him.

When you're facing tough times, follow Paul's example. Praise God for the comfort he's already promised, and then ask him to help you use your own experience to bring comfort to someone else.

Submit to God. Resist the devil and he will flee from you.

JAMES 4:7 NKJV

Battle Plan

The devil is referred to by many names throughout the Bible—accuser, tempter, deceiver, slanderer, enemy, Satan. One thing the Bible never calls him is a mythical creature. He is as real as God himself. There's no point in resisting someone who isn't there.

You need to know more, however, than that Satan exists. You need to know exactly what to do to defeat Satan. On the same day you aligned yourself with God, you gained this "adversary," which is what the word *Satan* literally means. Satan has no personal interest in you. His only aim

is to hurt God. One way he tries to do that is by trying to hurt the ones whom God loves. Satan is only a prideful, fallen angel. He isn't all-knowing or all-powerful. Yet he can still wreak havoc, causing you to doubt God's love or tempting you to go down the wrong road.

But you can stop Satan in his tracks. First, submit to God. In the original language, *submit* is a military command that means "to get into your proper rank." That's accomplished by humbly putting every aspect of your life under God's loving authority. Only then are you prepared to defeat the devil. *Resist* is also a military command that means "to stand bravely against." Stand against your adversary by recalling biblical truths. Strengthen your resolve through prayer. Turn your back on anything that entices you to turn away from God. Satan will flee from the battle before it has even begun.

> **Satan is only a prideful, fallen angel.**

Satan has no future. Jesus assured Satan's ultimate defeat by dying on the cross. The potential skirmishes that James alludes to are nothing more than diversionary tactics from an opponent who is destined to lose.

Those who love money will never have enough. How absurd to think that wealth brings true happiness! The more you have, the more people come to help you spend it. So what is the advantage of wealth—except perhaps to watch it run through your fingers!

ECCLESIASTES 5:10–11 NLT

Misguided Love

The book of Ecclesiastes includes one of the most important financial truths you'll ever hear. If you love money and the things it can buy, better budgeting, a higher-paying job, or even a winning lottery ticket can't make you happy or alleviate your financial worries. The only deciding factor that you can really depend on is to decide to pursue a fresh, new focus.

Love focuses on what it desires. When you desire God, you spend your time and energy getting to know him better and doing what pleases him. When you desire money, you spend your time and energy fueling an atmosphere of greed, instead of nurturing a sense of contentment. A deep desire for wealth can tempt you to do things you normally wouldn't consider, like cheating, lying, or stealing. You don't need to do anything illegal to fall for temptations like these. All it takes is holding on to the riches God has given you with a tight grip instead of opening

> **Pursuing riches more vigorously than a relationship with your God will lead you to only one place—an impoverished life.**

your arms, and hoarding your blessings instead of sharing them.

The book of Ecclesiastes is all about how meaningless life is apart from God. Pursuing riches more vigorously than a relationship with your God will lead you to only one place— an impoverished life. (Even if your bank account seems to say otherwise!) Instead of focusing on money, focus on God, the source of wealth. Thank him for how he has blessed you, and share what he has so generously given. You will find yourself rich in joy and contentment.

—110

Money promises more than it can ever deliver. God will never do that to you. The treasures he promises his children are both certain and eternal.

Trust in the LORD with all your heart, and lean not on your own understanding.

PROVERBS 3:5 NKJV

Leaning on the Lord

If you are going to lean on something, the first thing you want to do is to make certain it can hold you up. The greater the risk, the more certain you want to be. You may not test the strength of every chair you're considering sitting on, but it's fairly certain that you will test the integrity of a bungee cord before attaching it to your feet and leaping off a bridge. Your trust in the strength and reliability of the bungee cord allows you to lean on its ability to save you. It still may take a lot of courage to go ahead and jump, however.

Believing in God is all about risk and trust. It tells you to turn away from what you're accustomed to relying on—your own strategies for making life work—and instead to trust God implicitly, even when what he's asking you to do may not make sense from a human perspective. Think about what God asked of

Every past experience was once a present choice.

Moses at the Red Sea or of Daniel in the lions' den. Moses and Daniel were able to rely on God instead of on their own understanding because past experience had shown them he was wholly trustworthy.

Every past experience was once a present choice. God challenges you to choose wisely today. You can lean on your own limited understanding and abilities or on a God of unlimited power and love. Only one choice can take you where you really want to go.

Put what you've learned into practice. List why you believe God is trustworthy, focusing on his promises and past faithfulness. Reread the list anytime you need the courage to lean on him instead of on yourself.

Ｏne thing I always do. Forgetting the past and straining toward what is ahead, I keep trying to reach the goal and get the prize for which God called me through Christ to the life above.

PHILIPPIANS 3:13–14 NCV

Running to Win

When the apostle Paul said there is "one thing I always do," it is time to sit up and listen. Paul summarized his goal in life and shared a couple of quick tips on how to persevere toward reaching it. That makes his advice not only important, but extremely helpful to those with that same goal in mind.

Paul's images of "straining toward what is ahead" and "trying to reach the goal" paint a picture of a long-distance

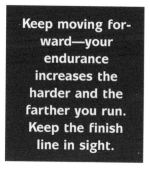

runner whose focus on the rewards of the finish line gives him the strength to persevere, one step at a time. The goal Paul pointed to is God's call to run toward a Jesus-centered life, leaving his self-centered life behind in the dust. The prize he longed to reach was not eternal life, because Jesus' death has already achieved that. Instead, Paul pursued a mature Christian life, one that yielded rewards both in heaven and on earth.

> **Keep moving forward—your endurance increases the harder and the farther you run. Keep the finish line in sight.**

Paul's purpose and process for perseverance provide practical applications you can use every day of your life. Put your past mistakes, victories, and self-reliance behind you. Focus your attention and energy on Jesus, not on those running the race alongside you. Keep moving forward—your endurance increases the harder and the farther you run. Keep the finish line in sight. It doesn't mark the end of your life; it marks the beginning of an eternity spent in the winner's circle with Jesus, the One who enables you to be victorious.

Persevering toward maturity in your faith takes both personal effort and the transforming power of God's Spirit. God works through you as you do his work.

Delight yourself also in the LORD, and He shall give you the desires of your heart.

PSALM 37:4 NKJV

Finding Your Heart's Desire

At first glance, the words from Psalm 37 feel a bit like a blank check. They seem to say, "Enjoy God and get everything you want." But instead of a promise of prosperity, the words are a proclamation of a profound truth: the closer you draw to God, the more your desires will reflect his own.

This oft-repeated verse is part of an acrostic psalm, where every other line begins with a successive letter of the Hebrew alphabet. Although each verse in Psalm 37 contains its own unique insight, all the verses work together to convey one important message. Those people who are wise have no need to worry during times of trouble. This psalm gives you four practical ways to defeat worry when evil people seem to be getting ahead: (1) trust in the Lord, (2) commit your way to the Lord, (3) wait on the Lord, and (4) delight in the Lord.

The focus of the psalmist's words is delighting in the Lord. The Hebrew word for *delight* is much more powerful than its English counterpart. Here it means "to find exquisite joy." To delight in God is to find your deepest pleasure, your highest ecstasy, and your richest fulfillment in life through your relationship with him. This is an ongoing process as you

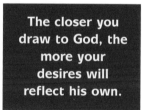

The closer you draw to God, the more your desires will reflect his own.

delight in him afresh each day. As your relationship deepens, what is dear to God's heart becomes dear to your heart. This aligns your prayers with God's will. As your prayers are answered, you discover that your deepest desires are fulfilled.

Any time you desire something that you know would also delight God, spend a moment thanking God for how he's helping you grow to be more like him.

Ｉn [Christ] all the treasures of wisdom and knowledge are safely kept.

COLOSSIANS 2:3 NCV

Buried Treasure

In ancient Colossae, Gnosticism was all the rage. It was a religious cult that promised salvation through secret knowledge that was said to be delivered by angels. Even the group's name was derived from the Greek word for "knowledge," *gnosis*. In his letter to the Colossians, Paul wanted the church to be able to discern what was false from what was true. Instead of seeking secret knowledge, Paul told people to seek Jesus—the source of knowledge itself.

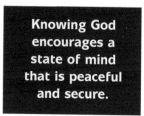

Today people continue to seek the answer to life through intellectual pursuits, philosophical debate, and even angelic revelation. Yet what was true in Paul's day is still true today. Faith in Jesus is the only road to salvation and to the secrets of life. Faith comes from knowing God through personal experience, not intellectual pursuit. Any knowledge derived from

> **Knowing God encourages a state of mind that is peaceful and secure.**

that perfect source bonds people together in love; they do not pit themselves against one another to show off what they know. Knowing God encourages a state of mind that is peaceful and secure.

Yet this kind of knowledge isn't a treasure trove you acquire the moment you invite God into your life. It is something that's revealed one gem at a time as you dig deeper into the Bible. Focus on Jesus. Get to know him intimately, with your whole being. You'll find knowledge that's practical, eternal, and worth infinitely more than any doctoral degree.

When you act on what you've learned by focusing on Jesus, you demonstrate wisdom. The more you put wisdom to use, the wiser you become.

God so loved the world that He gave His only begotten Son, that whoever believes in Him should not perish but have everlasting life.

JOHN 3:16 NKJV

The Never-Ending Story

John 3:16 has been nicknamed "the Little Gospel." That's because it condenses the message Jesus came to share into a single clear-cut sentence, answering one of the big questions every individual has to face: is there life after death? God's answer to that question is a resounding yes. That truly is "good news," which is what *gospel* literally means.

When you love someone, that love motivates you to give. The same is true with God. God loved the people of the world so deeply that he had to put that love into action. He did that by sending the very best gift he could ever give, a true part of himself—Jesus.

When you love someone, that love motivates you to give. The same is true with God.

Before any gift can be enjoyed, it has to be accepted. People accept God's gift by accepting who Jesus is. That's what belief is all about. But God doesn't stop there. Accepting Jesus comes with an extra bonus gift. That gift is a life that never ends. That gift isn't something people have to wait and open later. Its reality takes hold the moment people accept God's "good news" as a part of their lives. From that moment on, they experience a life that will not end with death but will continue beyond it as they grow ever closer to the One who loves them so deeply—and gave so much because of that love.

Consider a few of the countless ways God has shared his love with you. This generosity will extend from this life into the next. Take a few moments just to say thanks.

Be very careful how you live. Do not live like those who are not wise, but live wisely. Use every chance you have for doing good, because these are evil times.

EPHESIANS 5:15–16 NCV

Seize the Moment

Life is filled with opportunities—and obstacles that can prevent you from grabbing hold of them. The secret to making the most of your life lies in making the most of your time.

The first three words hold the key: *be very careful*. In the original language, this admonition is much stronger and fuller than what sounds here like a mother's passing comment to her kids as they head outside. The words describe a way of living (or "walking," as the Bible often describes it) that is precise, accurate, and deliberate. It involves both

forethought and a heightened sense of awareness. It's similar
to the way you drive a car. You need to
be constantly attentive, responding
appropriately to the ever-changing situations you find yourself in. You
swerve to avoid hazards, brake for
pedestrians, and follow the rules of the

> **You need to recognize evil, so you can avoid it like a dangerous hazard in the road.**

road. Your skill, knowledge, and vigilance help you make
wise decisions at a moment's notice.

To live wisely you need to do the same thing. You need
to face each day spiritually alert. You need to recognize evil,
so you can avoid it like a dangerous hazard in the road. At
the same time, you need to be on the lookout for opportunities to show love to others and to God—and to grab hold of
them. The good news is that God is in the car with you. His
Spirit will help guide your daily journey toward a life full of
well-utilized opportunities.

When you start your car, recall the words from the book of
Ephesians. They can be a reminder to keep your eyes open
for opportunities to make a positive difference throughout
your day.

God said to Moses, "I am who I am."

EXODUS 3:14 NKJV

What's in a Name?

To the people of Israel, a name was more than an identification for an individual. It was a statement about who that person was. When Moses (whose name means "taken from the water") met God for the first time via the burning bush, Moses wanted to know God's name. Moses wanted to know who God was. God's reply was "I am." Derived from the Hebrew verb *to be*, this name let Moses know that the One he was speaking to was unlike anyone else. God not only is, but he always was and always will be. God alone was never created, and he exists totally independent from anyone or anything else. "I am" is the one unchanging, eternal God.

The Jewish people considered God's name so holy that they refused to say it aloud for fear of using it in a way that dishonored him. In the New Testament, however, Jesus not only spoke God's name, but he also used it to refer to himself. The people listening immediately tried to stone Jesus. They knew God's words in Exodus. They understood that Jesus was calling himself God.

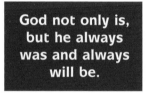

God not only is, but he always was and always will be.

When God told Moses his name, God revealed the essence of who he is—and confirmed in advance that the same essence was in his Son. In the same way that God introduced himself to Moses, this verse introduces you to God. It assures you that the "I am" of the universe is active and involved in life here on earth.

Understanding God's eternal nature, and that Jesus is wholly God, gives you the same assurance it did Moses. "I am" is with you, steadfast and unchangeable.

Let brotherly love continue. Do not forget to entertain strangers, for by so doing some have unwittingly entertained angels.

HEBREWS 13:1–2 NKJV

Open-Door Policy

In biblical times, practicing hospitality meant more than inviting your best friends over for dinner. Quite frequently it meant opening your door to a stranger. Long before mass transit, travelers often had to spend the night in an unfamiliar town as they journeyed from one place to another. In the early days of the church, many people were persecuted for their newfound faith in Jesus. Many were rejected by their families and in need of a place to stay. A practical way Christians loved one another was by extending their hospitality, often to those they'd never met. The Greek word for *hospitality* actually means "the love of strangers."

Today, though circumstances have changed, strangers are still in need of love. They may not show up unannounced at your door, but they are nearby if you simply open your eyes and your heart. A new neighbor, a visitor to your church, or even a child who needs foster care may be just the person God is asking you to make feel right at home.

The Bible says that even angels are occasional houseguests. This happened several times in the Old Testament to people like Abraham, Lot, and Gideon—and it could happen to you. However, angels are simply God's messengers. God uses people more frequently than angels when he wants to communicate

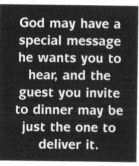

God may have a special message he wants you to hear, and the guest you invite to dinner may be just the one to deliver it.

with someone. God may have a special message he wants you to hear, and the guest you invite to dinner may be just the one to deliver it.

Pray God would help you become more aware of the people around you who could use your help, particularly those whom you don't know well. Ask one of them to dinner sometime this month.

Submit to one another out of reverence for Christ.

EPHESIANS 5:21 NLT

Willing Surrender

For many people, the idea of submitting themselves to someone else carries negative connotations. Submitting implies inferiority, subservience, or blind obedience. Nothing could be farther from God's truth. Submission as described in the Bible is a mutual commitment between two equals whose goal is to foster unity and cooperation. The ancient Greek word used in the Bible to describe submission is a military command telling troops to get in order according to their rank. By following this structure of authority, soldiers can work together more efficiently to

accomplish their own individual duties. A company with too many generals and not enough privates has little chance of winning a war.

In the Bible, several verses ask wives to submit to their husbands, servants to submit to their masters, and citizens to submit to the government. Ephesians 5:21 lays the groundwork for them all. It makes absolutely clear that submission is expected of every follower of Jesus, not just a few specific groups of people. One way that Jesus showed his love was by willingly setting his rights aside to better serve others. Every time you follow his example, you honor him.

> In daily life, submitting to one another looks a lot like respect, humility, and love.

In daily life, submitting to one another looks a lot like respect, humility, and love. It means that demanding your own way, flaunting your authority, or nurturing a superiority complex are things of the past. It means that your life is beginning to look more like Jesus'.

Before mutual submission is evident in your actions, it needs to take root in your attitude. That process begins the moment you submit your own personal agenda for life to God's.

73

Jesus said to those Jews who believed Him, "If you abide in My word, you are My disciples indeed. And you shall know the truth, and the truth shall make you free."

JOHN 8:31–32 NKJV

Free at Last

In today's postmodern society, talking about truth can be tricky. If you want to discuss *a* truth, feel free. However, talking about *the* truth is a whole other matter. Talking about the truth would imply that what you're sharing is an absolute truth, something that is true for everyone— whether everyone personally believes it to be true or not.

That's the kind of truth Jesus was talking about to his Jewish audience in the temple treasury as recorded in the Gospel of John. The term Jesus used for *truth* was the same

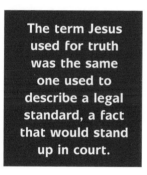

one used to describe a legal standard, a fact that would stand up in court. This fact was broader than just the truth about who Jesus was. The Jews who were listening already believed. The truth Jesus spoke of is the kind revealed over the course of a lifetime, as those who believe in him choose to obey his words.

In ancient Greek, *know* means more than "to make a mental note of." It means that you have tested your belief experientially. By putting Jesus' teaching into practice, you can come to know the truth about God, life, and yourself. This knowledge frees you from chains you may not even be aware are holding you back, such chains as pride, selfishness, and the temptation to do what is contrary to Jesus' words. Let God's truth lead you to true freedom today.

> **The term Jesus used for truth was the same one used to describe a legal standard, a fact that would stand up in court.**

God's promise of freedom is linked to putting his words to the test. Get to know his words better by reading, meditating on, and praying about at least one verse of Scripture each day.

IMPORTANT BIBLE VERSES FOR MEN

He who has begun a good work in you will complete it until the day of Jesus Christ.

PHILIPPIANS 1:6 NKJV

He who has seen Me has seen the Father.

JOHN 14:9 NKJV

God and Man

Jesus was a man, just like you. He was born, grew up, learned how to make a living, and worked for a number of years. He got hungry and ate, got thirsty and drank, got tired and slept. He traveled around, made friends, and eventually made his mark on the world. When he died, he was buried just like any other man.

But this ordinary guy made a very important claim: that he was God in person, that anyone who observed him would know what God is like. He backed up this claim as well, performing miracles with the power of God, teaching with the wisdom of God, reaching out to outcasts with the compassion of God, and forgiving people's wrongs with the authority of God.

Jesus was a man, and yet when he commanded a storm to cease, the wind and the waves complied. He was a human being, and yet when he spoke to the mob who came to arrest him, the entire throng fell to the ground. Jesus was made of flesh

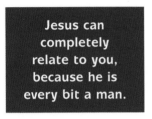

Jesus can completely relate to you, because he is every bit a man.

and blood, and yet on the third day after they laid his body in a tomb, he walked right back out. Jesus can completely relate to you, because he is every bit a man. He can also teach you a lot about God, as he is every bit God himself. Simply watch what he does and listen to what he says.

⁓⁑⊙

Jesus' life was well documented; the New Testament in the Bible chronicles his words and his actions. Make a commitment to learn all you can about him, so you'll begin to understand God.

Every promise of the LORD your God has come true. Not a single one has failed!

JOSHUA 23:14 NLT

Signed Contract

When a man signs a contract, he literally puts his name on the line. He makes a written vow to perform in some manner, perhaps to deliver goods or services or pay for them. As he conscientiously follows through on his obligation, he establishes good credit and goodwill. People trust him and want to continue doing business with him.

God put his pledges in writing. He was willing to risk his reputation, which he highly values, by having his promises recorded in the pages of the Bible. They're right there

in black and white for every man to see. God has already fulfilled many of them, and the details of how he did so have been similarly recorded. He certainly wouldn't mind if you checked it all out for yourself.

One thing about God is, he never changes. If your examination of his "credit history" indicates a pattern of promises made and promises kept, you can be sure he will remain reliable. Then you can focus on his promises to you. Many of the pledges that God made to individuals

> **Many of the pledges that God made to individuals long ago have implications for you today.**

long ago have implications for you today, but some were limited to a specific person, time, and place. It's important not only to know what God's promises to you are but also to understand them well. Once you do, you'll find they're almost too good to be true. Yet don't forget who signed his name under each one.

God is always willing to do business with a man willing to deal with him. Learn all you can about the great promises he offers you, and determine to take him up on each one. (See Matthew 5:3–10; Proverbs 3:5–6; Jeremiah 17:7–8; Deuteronomy 31:8; Psalm 128:1–4.)

God has chosen you and made you his holy people. He loves you. So always do these things: Show mercy to others, be kind, humble, gentle, and patient.

COLOSSIANS 3:12 NCV

Nice Guys

Men today are striving to reclaim their manhood; they're trying to learn what it means to be strong, to be assertive, to be a man according to God's standards. They no longer want to be thought of simply as nice guys. But in this admirable search for authentic masculinity, there's a danger that men will abandon the quieter virtues of manhood for those that are more dramatic.

God *is* calling you to be a real man. He has singled you out because he loves you, and he will teach you how to become a man in every sense. That's partly why he sent Jesus into the world: to provide you with a model of perfect manliness. Jesus was the greatest man who ever lived. There was a fathomless strength to his character. He was bold enough to criticize influential people, and forceful enough to drive away everyone who was using God's temple as a marketplace. But he was more than simply

> **God designed you to be a nice guy.**

a powerful guy. He was also a man who was warm-hearted and sympathetic, never hesitant to show his soft, caring side.

If you're going to be a true man, you will need all the virtues God intended men to possess. God designed you to be a nice guy. He meant for you to have a kindly quality about you, undergirded by the inner strength and drive to fulfill all of his purposes for your life.

─❧❧─

Work hard to acquire every virtue of authentic masculinity. It may seem like trying to move in several directions at once, but God will make it possible for you to attain all these attributes.

Those who worship hollow gods,
god-frauds, walk away from their only
true love. But I'm worshiping you, GOD,
calling out in thanksgiving!

JONAH 2:8–9 MSG

Man's Greatest Love

The only true love a man has ever known—love that is pure, unconditional, steadfast, and everlasting—has come from God. He has loved you longer and stronger than anyone has, more than your parents, your friends, your wife, your children, or anybody else. God's love has been coming your way since before you were conceived, and regardless of how you've responded to him or what kinds of decisions you've made over the years, it has never let up for an instant.

However, God has felt the pain of separation every time you've been distracted from him by the people and things in your life. Any father would suffer greatly if his son poured all his affection into sports and school and friends and music and movies and computers and video games. All these are fine

> The greatest love a man will ever experience is the bond between himself and God.

with a father—until they interfere with his relationship with his son. That is of utmost importance to him.

The greatest love a man will ever experience is the bond between himself and God. When you honor God's perfect love for you by putting your relationship with him above all else and revering him alone, your connection with him will remain strong. You'll find that the love you share with God is more exciting, vital, and fulfilling than anything else in your life. Your relationships with others will thrive because of it, and you'll enjoy all of God's gifts to you with deep gratitude and delight.

~⁂~

Are you communicating with God in prayer regularly? Do you find that you're increasingly aware of his presence each day? These are the surest signs that you are being true to your greatest love.

"You shall love the LORD your God with all your heart, with all your soul, with all your mind, and with all your strength." This is the first commandment.

MARK 12:30 NKJV

Life's Focus

Can you imagine what it would be like to work on a carving like Mount Rushmore? Suspended high on the face of a cliff, you'd have to keep the big picture in perspective while chipping away at the rock inches in front of you. Somehow you'd have to focus on two things at once: what you're doing at the moment, and ultimately why you're doing it.

That's not much different from a man's everyday life. Each day presents a mountain of ways to expend your passion, time, and energy, and you have to determine where you're going to chisel. The decision is much easier when you can see the big picture clearly and understand what matters most in life. That will help you set your priorities straight.

Jesus knew that life's most important purpose is to love God, and that's where he concentrated his effort. By following Jesus' example, you'll make

> **By following Jesus' example, you'll make the right choices.**

the right choices. Your life will take on a shape that exhibits your love for God, and it will stand forever as a monument to him.

Did you know that in the game of chess, all the pieces have a numerical value except the king? That's because he's invaluable. Every other piece has its function and worth, but falls into its respective rank after him. The king is the whole object of the game, and a wise player keeps him in focus at all times. Make God your highest priority, and all the other areas of your life will fall nicely into place.

If you are searching for meaning in your life, invite God into it and make him your focal point. Give God top priority, because he gives everything else purpose.

Accept each other just as Christ has accepted you.

ROMANS 15:7 NLT

Join
the Club

Jesus had a reputation for being a "friend of sinners." He was perfectly willing to hang around with people who were less than perfect. It's a good thing he was, because according to the Bible, every man falls into that category. However, the Bible also says that people carry the imprint of God in their very being. Jesus was able to look beyond everyone's defects and recognize their basic humanity. He never prejudged or stereotyped people, but rather approached them as individuals who were worthy of dignity and respect just because God made them and loved them.

There's a lot of truth to the saying "Nobody's perfect." Jesus, being God, is the only exception to that rule. He is also the only person in a position to judge anyone. He reached out to you, *knowing* you were truly beneath him, so it's essential that you extend your hand to those you only *think* aren't as good as you.

> **Jesus was able to look beyond everyone's defects and recognize their basic humanity.**

Remember what it cost God to embrace you as a friend. Since God is absolutely perfect, the only way he could have a relationship with you was to find a way to get rid of all your imperfections. He accomplished that through Jesus' death on the cross. If God sacrificed so much to welcome you into his presence, why not give up a little pride and be willing to associate with all of his children? They may seem flawed, but the cross offers hope that God will one day make them perfect.

⸺⟩

Start making an effort to befriend people whom others have rejected. You'll soon have quite a rep yourself—as a man who is just like Jesus. That's the best reputation you could ever earn.

N̲o̲ one who trusts God like this—heart and soul—will ever regret it.

ROMANS 10:11 MSG

No Regrets

If you're like most men, you want to live life with no regrets. When you reach the end of the line, you want to be able to look back and feel that you've experienced life fully, that you haven't missed out on anything. In the final analysis, you want to feel that you haven't made any big mistakes you could have avoided. You want to believe that you've made the best of your opportunities in life.

The Bible says that if you put your complete confidence in God, trusting him fully in every area of your life and tak-

ing him at his word for all your needs, you'll never be sorry. You won't spend your final hours on earth wishing you would've put a little more faith in other things, such as money. Just the opposite. You'll reflect on your life and realize it was rich in a way you never dreamed possible, and that believing in God's promises was the best decision you ever could have made.

> **It's not too late to shift your confidence to where it needs to be today.**

No matter how much time you have left in this world, it's imperative to choose right now where to stake your future. You may have some regrets from misplacing your trust in the past, but it's not too late to shift your confidence to where it needs to be today. If you pick wisely and through prayer commit yourself totally into God's hands, you'll have every reason to celebrate your choice from now until the end of your life.

—⟩⟩⟩○

If you haven't trusted God before or have trusted him only a little, begin putting *all* your faith in him today. It's an entirely different way to live—yet there's no better way to go.

Without faith it is impossible to please Him, for he who comes to God must believe that He is, and that He is a rewarder of those who diligently seek Him.

HEBREWS 11:6 NKJV

The Key to It All

There's a reason why the words *LORD* and *GOD* often appear in capital letters in the Bible. Modern translations of the Bible use these words to indicate where the actual name of God is found in the original manuscripts. Ancient scribes used a special font when they hand-copied this name onto their parchments. In the Dead Sea Scrolls, for instance, God's name stands out from the rest of the text, just as on the pages of a Bible. It was the name God told Moses at the burning bush, and it was considered so holy that for a long time people were afraid to say it aloud. Today no one is certain how it was pronounced. Its meaning, however, is very clear: God's name is "I AM."

The essence of faith is taking God at his word. Faith at its root is a man's agreeing with God, accepting that what he says is true. It begins with

> **Trusting God is the key to every man's relationship with him.**

God's name, which addresses the core issue of whether or not "he is." With all the science and technology available in the twenty-first century, there's still no way to prove or disprove God's existence. You must rely on his word.

Trusting God is the key to every man's relationship with him. It's the crucial element in knowing him and earning his favor. God declares he is real. If you believe this and everything else he says, and search for him wholeheartedly, you'll be lavishly compensated: you'll find him, and all his promises will bear your name.

~∭◦

The commonsense approach to life is to first see proof, then believe. But above all, God wants every man to trust him. Believe God's words; he will prove himself to you and reward your faith.

You can't worship God and Money both.

Matthew 6:24 msg

Got to Choose

By and large, today's money is nothing more than bits of electronic data stored in some computer somewhere. If the computer at your bank finds the right sequence of bits for your account, it will approve a purchase. Scrooge McDuck would get quite a jolt if he tried to wallow in that kind of currency. If you find you're putting more thought and energy into building up your bank accounts than cultivating your relationship with God, take a moment and think about exactly what you're dedicating your life to.

Nobody loves money for what it is; a man loves money for what it can do. Money represents purchasing power, the power to buy whatever you want to buy, go wherever you want to go, and do whatever you want to do. So the hard truth is that worshiping and serving money equates to living for yourself rather than for God. Fortunately, there's a way out of that trap, by making God your Master and money your servant.

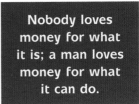

Nobody loves money for what it is; a man loves money for what it can do.

Money has many honorable functions in the life of a man who's wholeheartedly committed to God. It enables you to purchase the things you and your family need, as well as supply other people's needs through charitable giving. If you submit yourself to God and gain control over your budget, money can free up your schedule so you'll have more time for him and others. Choose the right master, and your life will truly be enriched.

Men are great at compartmentalizing their lives, but God and money require different approaches. Instead of trying to juggle them separately, focus on God and let him teach you how to handle your finances.

We are His workmanship, created in Christ Jesus for good works, which God prepared beforehand that we should walk in them.

EPHESIANS 2:10 NKJV

Positive Energy

Some guys think God takes all the happiness out of life by stamping every wonder he created with an "Off Limits" sign. But living God's way is less about avoiding bad things than it is about doing what's more worthwhile. God's purpose isn't to ruin your fun; it's to add meaning and joy to your existence. If your experience with God has lacked vitality, try shifting your focus off his *don'ts* and onto his *dos*. It'll put wind in your sails.

Every man's goal should be to become what God intends him to be, and to accomplish what God means him to do. These objectives will start your heart pumping, get you out of bed, and get you going. And as God's *dos* (such as his command to serve him wholeheartedly) give you forward momentum, you'll realize that all of his *don'ts* (such as his warning not to make possessions your focus) are meant to keep you from getting bogged down.

> An ordinary man serving God is extraordinary indeed.

God may have designed you to be someone great or planned for you to be a regular guy. Becoming the latter may not sound very inspiring, but an ordinary man serving God is extraordinary indeed. God often uses common people to achieve mighty things. The work God has in mind for you may run the gamut from everyday good deeds to outstanding great works. It's all important to God. Any life lived for his purposes is highly significant, and choosing that goal will set your heart on fire.

~

Find and fulfill your purpose in life by connecting more intimately with Jesus. Build your relationship with him to discover who you are and receive the power to become it.

We do not lose heart. Even though our outward man is perishing, yet the inward man is being renewed day by day.

2 Corinthians 4:16 NKJV

Gray Hairs

Television sitcoms poke a lot of fun at middle-aged guys trying to cling to their youth by coloring their hair, combing over their bald spots, wearing toupees, and tightening their belts. Although these characters are laughable, you have to admire their spunk. Everyone knows they're fighting a losing battle, but their eternal optimism keeps them going.

Thankfully, God offers you a better hope than this. It's true that you're on the same road as every other man physically, whether you're in your prime, just over the hill, or well along in the aging process. But as the apostle Paul reminded the Corinthians, if you invite God's Spirit to live in you, then your inner self—the real you, the part of you that lasts for-ever—will be made brand-new every day of your life. Not only that, but when you allow God into your heart, he will start changing you on the inside, and he will continue to improve you until you join him in heaven, at which point you'll be perfect. Talk about the prime of your life!

> **If you invite God's Spirit to live in you, then your inner self— the real you, the part of you that lasts forever— will be made brand-new every day of your life.**

With God you'll grow older *and* better. You can color your hair if you want to, but God sees gray hair as a crown of honor. Why not wear it proudly? Despite all the emphasis modern culture places on youth, a man whose self-identity and self-esteem are rooted in his relationship with God can choose to age with dignity and grace.

~ⅢⒻ

Participate daily in God's renovating work inside you. Allow God to replace your old, wrong patterns of thinking and behaving with right ones, and you'll feel more and more like a new man.

Though you do not see him, you trust him; and even now you are happy with a glorious, inexpressible joy.

1 PETER 1:8 NLT

No Greater Delight

Some events in a man's life evoke feelings of bliss. One is falling in love, winning the heart of the girl you're crazy about. Another is becoming a father, seeing for the first time the child God has given you and falling in love all over again. And then there is achieving a dream, accomplishing the goal you've had your heart set on for years.

If you've known any of these blessings, you have an inkling of the flood of joy that God begins to pour out on a man who decides to follow him. That's because each of these experiences reflects a different quality of the best event that could occur in any man's life—becoming a Christian.

Think of what it means to put your confidence in God. You've never laid eyes on God; no portrait or photograph or even physical description exists. Yet you get to know him, come to adore him, and choose to join your life with his forever. Like falling in love. You realize that this new person in your life is the most awesome, precious gift you've ever received. Like becoming a father. And the longer you walk with God, the more excited and jubilant

The longer you walk with God, the more excited and jubilant you feel, because you know you're moving ever closer to a fantastic destination.

you feel, because you know you're moving ever closer to a fantastic destination. Like achieving a dream. Recognizing that God brings such enduring, expanding, exhilarating joy is one of the most compelling reasons for a man to believe in him.

⸺⟡⸻

Trust God, allow your spirit to respond joyfully to his presence, and as a blind man learns to use his remaining senses to perceive others, more and more you'll "see" him.

Put yourself aside, and help others get ahead. Don't be obsessed with getting your own advantage. Forget yourselves long enough to lend a helping hand.

PHILIPPIANS 2:3–4 MSG

Looking Out for Number Two

Everybody wants a better job, a bigger home, a nicer car. Nowadays these things come and go quickly. Employees frequently switch jobs and companies throughout their careers. People live in a house five or six years and then move on. And many cars are driven only a short time before their owners sell them or trade them in. Amid all this upward mobility, God is calling men to a much higher standard of living.

One of the strongest themes in the Bible is the call to look out for the well-being of others. As you tend to your career and your personal affairs, learn to replace selfish ambition with godly ambition.

Other people will soon need your job, your house, and your car. Look out for their interests by being responsible with these things while you possess them, and by showing integrity as you transfer ownership. Take good care of your car and home, keep maintenance records, and be honest and fair when you sell. Likewise, do your job to the best of your ability, keep your files in order, and train your replacement well, helping to ensure his or her success. One day you may even decide to step aside and let someone else move ahead. Trust that anytime you're looking out for the other guy, God is looking out for you.

> **Trust that anytime you're looking out for the other guy, God is looking out for you.**

Make a commitment to always consider others' welfare as well as — or instead of — your own. Ask God to help you trade your ambition for his, and trust him to look after your well-being.

May our Lord Jesus Christ Himself, and our God and Father, who has loved us and given us everlasting consolation and good hope by grace, comfort your hearts and establish you in every good word and work.

2 THESSALONIANS 2:16–17 NKJV

Moral Support

Every man needs encouragement as he tries to live a godly life, especially if he's in an environment that offers little moral support. Perhaps the code of ethics at your workplace falls short of the Bible's standards for integrity. You may notice other employees acting dishonestly; your own boss may ask you to lie to clients to protect the bottom line. God will stand behind you in such a situation, urging you to hold tightly to your convictions.

When you feel as if you're alone on the gridiron in a hostile stadium, surrounded by the other team's colors and by voices of opposition, pray to God for support. He will reassure you of his presence and affirm your desire to do what's right. You'll know in your heart that he is close at hand, and that knowledge will fill you with hope and strength of purpose. It will give you the confidence you need to press on.

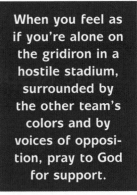

When you feel as if you're alone on the gridiron in a hostile stadium, surrounded by the other team's colors and by voices of opposition, pray to God for support.

God will encourage you in other ways as well. When the prophet Elijah hid in the desert, thinking he was all alone in the world, God told him that in fact there were seven thousand godly people in Israel. God will help you see that you're not alone either. You'll look around the field and discover that you're surrounded by teammates whose hearts beat true.

God will always be there to spur you on.

Strive to live according to God's principles, and look to him for encouragement when it seems you're the only one who does. God will always be there to spur you on.

Fear this glorious and awesome name,
THE LORD YOUR GOD.

DEUTERONOMY 28:58 NKJV

Due Respect

As a man learns about what God is like and about the wonderful things God has done for people through the ages, and as he experiences God more and more in his own life, he will realize that God has earned a spectacular reputation. God has made a name for himself that stands alone. It is distinguished, distinct from every other name. And that's precisely what the Bible means when it describes God's name—and God himself—as *holy*: set apart, unique, exceptional.

God's name has been misused throughout time. Men have degraded it by using it frivolously or, even more inconceivable, invoking it as a curse. Also, many who have claimed to represent God have sullied his good name through words and actions that aren't in line with his character. But God cares a great deal about his reputation and his name, and he will always see to it that they are polished off and reestablished to their proper height, where they reflect the reality of who he is.

> **If you love God, you'll contend for his honor most fiercely of all.**

A man will stand to defend his own reputation, the honor of his family, the name of a close friend. If you love God, you'll contend for his honor most fiercely of all. But before you can do that with integrity, you must be certain that in every way you are revering his name. This involves veneration, esteem, respect, even a healthy sense of fear. God's name is majestic, and it is always to be held in the highest regard.

⁓⁂⁐

God promises that if you honor him, he will honor you. Are you upholding his name in everything you think, say, and do? What are some ways you could treat God's name with more respect?

Be careful and guard against all kinds of greed. Life is not measured by how much one owns.

Luke 12:15 NCV

Not Good

Michael Douglas's character in the movie *Wall Street* declared that greed was good. He may have put it a little bluntly, but on some level was he right? As capitalism continues to spread around the world, it's easy to get the impression that life is all about accumulating as much wealth and property as possible. Doing otherwise seems wrong. If a man goes through a time when all he can afford to do is maintain the status quo—he can't buy a new house, remodel his current home, trade in his car, or purchase anything that

isn't a necessity—he feels as if his life is going nowhere. And "downsizing" seems downright unnatural.

In today's world the desire to acquire seems acceptable, just part of life. It's time to stop and take another look at this issue. If you really want to know what life is all about, you've got to get God's perspective on things. Only he has a handle on the real facts of life. And the truth is, greed is *not* good. The hunt

> **The hunt for more, more, more is simply not a man's purpose for living.**

for more, more, more is simply not a man's purpose for living. Jesus pointedly asked his listeners what good it would do to gain the whole world yet lose your soul.

God created men to be much more than ruthless tycoons or insatiable consumers. Your life doesn't reside in your bank account or your investments or your belongings; it resides in your relationship with him.

~

Employ a man's best weapon against greed: giving. Share whatever amount of wealth God has given you with the needy. Instead of unhealthy desire, you'll experience a wholesome sense of peace, well-being, and satisfaction.

Go therefore and make disciples of all the nations, baptizing them in the name of the Father and of the Son and of the Holy Spirit, teaching them to observe all things that I have commanded you; and lo, I am with you always, even to the end of the age.

MATTHEW 28:19–20 NKJV

Mission Statement

Many men attempt to clarify their purpose in life by crafting a personal mission statement. This helps them determine the reason for their existence and focus on fulfilling it. After Jesus died on the cross and rose again—achieving his own purpose on earth, to provide everlasting life for everyone who believes in him—he gave his followers a clear-cut mission statement: to tell everybody in the world what he had done and invite them to follow him.

Every man needs to incorporate into his personal mission statement the essence of Jesus' command, known as the Great Commission. However, the way this will shape each man's life will vary. Adopting the Great Commission inspires some guys to stand on street corners, some to go door-to-door, some to travel to foreign countries. It may motivate you to talk about Jesus with the people you care about most, such as family members, coworkers, and friends.

Doing your part to fulfill the Great Commission involves risk, often to valued relationships. And it means more than just telling people about Jesus and walking away. It's about creating followers of Jesus, and that also requires helping people to make a formal commitment to him and teaching them to obey him. Finally, it's something no

Doing your part to fulfill the Great Commission involves risk, often to valued relationships.

man can do alone. After issuing the Great Commission, Jesus made an equally great promise: to always be with you so you can accomplish it. He will go wherever you go, helping you achieve his final command.

Make it your mission to tell others about who Jesus is, what he did, and what he taught, and to encourage them to follow him. It's one of the most significant purposes of your life.

I have filled him with the Spirit of God, in wisdom, in understanding, in knowledge, and in all manner of workmanship.

EXODUS 31:3 NKJV

God-Given Talents

Men display an incredible range of talents. You see this all around—in business, sports, science, medicine, the arts. It's amazing what guys can do. Where does all this ability come from? The Bible says it comes straight from God.

This truth is seen in Bezalel, the man God chose to head construction of the tabernacle, a large tent in which the Israelites could worship God as they crossed the desert. God gave Bezalel extraordinary capability in working with metal, wood, and stone. He was a master craftsman and designer, and he was able to teach others. God empowered

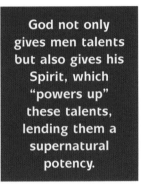

Bezalel for one important reason: to build the structure God envisioned.

Bezalel's story teaches four crucial points. Two are overt, and two lie just below the surface. First, God gives men aptitude and wisdom. Some of it is hardwired at conception; some is acquired through education and experience. However, God orchestrates the whole process. He makes men and molds them. Second, God not only gives men talents but also gives his Spirit, which "powers up" these talents, lending

> **God not only gives men talents but also gives his Spirit, which "powers up" these talents, lending them a supernatural potency.**

them a supernatural potency. Third, God has specific intentions when he doles out abilities. They are meant to be used for his lofty purposes. Finally, if God's purposes are to be accomplished, the man receiving these gifts must be willing to use them for God's glory—by doing the work God is calling him to do. If God's tabernacle was to be built, Bezalel had to set hammer to chisel.

God has given you a unique blend of skill, ability, and knowledge. Thank him for all your gifts, ask him to show you their purpose, and be willing to use them to achieve it.

Is there anyplace I can go to avoid your Spirit? To be out of your sight? If I climb to the sky, you're there! If I go underground, you're there! If I flew on morning's wings to the far western horizon, you'd find me in a minute—you're already there waiting!

PSALM 139:7–10 MSG

Universal Coverage

God is omnipresent—he is everywhere all the time. No matter where a man goes, God is with him. Your cell phone company may be good, but it can't guarantee coverage like that. God is always right there beside you. This is true whether or not you sense his presence, just as a strong mobile phone signal in a well-covered area is present regardless of whether or not your cell phone is on.

This fact has two important ramifications for every man. The first is that no matter how hard you try, you can't hide from God. He sees everything you do. Incidentally, he also knows everything you think, so you can't fool him either. The thought of always being clearly in God's view may make you feel uncomfortable and guilty—God often has that effect on men, once they're aware that he really is watching them. If so, your best response is to run toward God. You'll find that he is not only always around but also always willing to forgive.

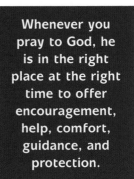

Whenever you pray to God, he is in the right place at the right time to offer encouragement, help, comfort, guidance, and protection.

The second ramification of God's steadfast presence is that he is always immediately available to you. He hears a man as well as sees him. Whenever you pray to God, he is in the right place at the right time to offer encouragement, help, comfort, guidance, and protection. There is no place in the universe you can go where he can't be there for you.

Remind yourself every morning of God's constant nearness. Make your awareness of it a source of joy for you all day long, and allow yourself to bask in his presence.

117

Godliness with contentment is great gain.

1 TIMOTHY 6:6 NKJV

This Is the Life

Grasping the wisdom of this short verse is like hitting the power button on your remote control in the middle of a sports car commercial. Immediately everything changes. One moment your mind is consumed with the best the world has to offer—beauty, speed, luxury, prestige—the next all is peaceful and quiet. The advertiser's busy, noisy attempts to make you discontented with your life are silenced, and you're free to feel satisfied with all the blessings God has given you.

Understanding the apostle Paul's message to Timothy is vital to living the rich life God intends for you, because it reveals the true meaning of the word *profit*. Every man has a desire to advance, make progress, improve his lot. Madison Avenue offers the world's definition of *achievement*; Paul provides God's. Embrace the latter, and your life will take on new direction. Like a running back reorienting himself in a chaotic play, you'll turn and begin striving for the right goal.

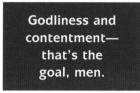

Godliness and contentment— that's the goal, men.

Godliness and contentment—that's the goal, men. Marketing gurus say that if you can acquire it all, you'll be content. The Bible says that if you're godly and content, you already have it all. The clincher, the truly amazing thing about the life God offers, is that even when you have it all, he continues to pour on blessings. Jesus promised that if you make godliness and contentment your aim, your heavenly Father will give you everything you need. That's the abundant life God wants to give you.

Develop godly contentment by focusing on your gratitude for all God's gifts. Ask God to teach you what true contentment is—not complacency but a condition of the heart that motivates you toward great deeds.

As far as the east is from the west, so far has He removed our transgressions from us.

PSALM 103:12 NKJV

Clean Slate

Guilt has two guises. It can be a fact or a feeling. A young man working part-time at a grocery store is guilty in fact if he takes snacks off the shelf to eat during his breaks. He may not *feel* guilty about it; perhaps he's new on the job, notices other employees doing it, and despite the tug of his conscience figures the store owner won't mind. However, the fact remains that he's stealing, breaking the law.

What if the young man sees his coworkers get caught, lose their jobs, and face prosecution for employee theft? Now, in addition to being guilty, he may feel shame and

remorse. He may have a hard time looking the store owner in the eye. When the disciple Peter denied twice that he ever knew Jesus, he committed two grave offenses. Yet it wasn't until the third time, when Jesus caught his eye, that Peter realized the magnitude of what he'd done and wept bitterly.

Jesus completely forgave Peter. The great thing about God's promise to remove your guilt just as thoroughly is that it applies to both fact and feeling. God will deal with the root of any guilty emotions you may be

> **Whatever your offense, God will eliminate it from the record entirely, restoring your sense of innocence.**

carrying around, if you admit to him that you did wrong. Whatever your offense, God will eliminate it from the record entirely, restoring your sense of innocence. He will also help you face the consequences of your actions and make amends, so your earthly slate will be clean too.

When God wipes a man's slate clean, it is clean indeed. Are you burdened with guilt? Ask God to forgive you and help you set things right, and then trust him to completely forget whatever wrong you committed.

The Spirit produces the fruit of love, joy, peace, patience, kindness, goodness, faithfulness, gentleness, self-control.

GALATIANS 5:22–23 NCV

Help with the Reins

A man's spirit is like a stallion that always wants to run wild. You need a lot of will power to bridle your spirit and make it obedient to God. Of course, if running wild produced a life of joy and contentment, there'd be no incentive for you to even try to restrain your urges and desires. But it's been said that discipline is freedom. The only way to experience true liberty and happiness is to gain control over the mustang inside you, and bring yourself into compliance with God's way of living.

How can you master such a willful beast? In the study of literature, conflict is classified into categories such as man against nature or man against man. In this case it's man against himself. Sometimes the hardest thing in the world to do is fight your own impulses. They can be so strong that it seems unnatural to deny them. It feels wrong to do the right thing. The key to winning this battle is to become so familiar with God's ways that you can recognize the difference between right and wrong despite your feelings.

The only way to experience true liberty and happiness is to gain control over the mustang inside you.

Study the Bible thoroughly, and listen for God's voice whenever you're struggling with self-control. He will tell you clearly what you need to do, and then if you ask him, he will step into the fray and help you do it. Self-control is a misnomer, really; it's impossible to do it alone. Let God give you a hand with the reins.

Ask God each day for the gift of self-control. It's a good gift, and it brings with it many other good gifts such as love and peace and goodness and joy.

The righteous man walks in his integrity;
his children are blessed after him.

PROVERBS 20:7 NKJV

A Rich Legacy

When a man holds his child for the first time, he feels a powerful desire to be a good father. He begins to think about the kind of legacy he will pass on to his child. He knows that if he can be a good father, he'll leave behind not merely an investment portfolio but an inheritance that will enrich his child's life emotionally and spiritually, and similarly touch the lives of generations to follow.

According to the book of Proverbs, the key to being a good father is to be a good man. Your children will have a

rich heritage if your life is above reproach. That's a tall order, but you can live faultlessly by maintaining an intimate relationship with your own heavenly Father. Through the Bible and his Spirit, God will teach you how to live a blameless life, and empower you to do it. If you cooperate with him, your children will profit enormously.

Living blamelessly means making a one-time, whole-hearted commitment to obey God, then continually choosing to obey him for the rest of your life. It also involves always admitting to God any disobedi-

> **The key to being a good father is to be a good man.**

ence and getting right back in step with him. God will take away your guilt the moment you do, for he holds nothing against a man trying his best to obey him and asking for forgiveness whenever he fails. Such a man is deemed good, and his children will receive a tremendous inheritance— including an invaluable role model for their lives.

Do you really want to be a good father? Focus on being a good man. Commit yourself to living God's way, seek forgiveness for your mistakes, and he will reward both you and your children.

The LORD shall preserve you from all evil;
He shall preserve your soul.

PSALM 121:7 NKJV

Ultimate Security

Where should a man's sense of security be invested? In the government and the police? In a home-security system? In a gun next to his bed? During biblical times, the people of Israel were constantly placing their confidence in kings, armies, protective walls, and weapons. Again and again God showed them that he was their true source of security.

When God told an Israelite named Gideon to defend his people against the hordes of enemies encamped in their lands, Gideon raised up an army of more than thirty thousand men. But God whittled Gideon's forces down to just three hundred, so the Israelites would know that it was God who had saved them. In another instance, God acted alone, simply wiping out a huge enemy army overnight. At such times there was no doubt who Israel's protector was.

Men should take steps to ensure the safety of their nation, their communities, and their homes. However, God declares that unless he is in the picture, those trying

> **Only God can guarantee protection.**

to provide security are wasting their time. Only God can guarantee protection. As the preeminent guard in your life, God will help you look after your wife, your children, and your property. God, who never sleeps, will be vigilant twenty-four hours a day. He will provide you and your loved ones with ultimate security: freedom from worry and fear in this lifetime, and a carefree existence with him ever after.

~

Invest your sense of security in God. Pray daily, thanking him for his protection and asking him to continue watching over you and yours. You'll breathe a lot easier, and sleep much better.

We also have joy with our troubles, because we know that these troubles produce patience. And patience produces character, and character produces hope.

ROMANS 5:3–4 NCV

End Product

A debilitating injury can strike a man hard, causing him to suffer not only physically but also emotionally, by attacking his sense of self-worth. However, God can use such times of pain so that rather than breaking you, they make you stronger, and instead of causing you to despair, they create in you a rock-solid optimism. One of the most wonderful traits of God is his ability to take the black coal of suffering and transform it into the shining diamond of hope.

If you turn to God for help when you're hurting, he does much more than comfort you. He gives you the fortitude you need to bear pain courageously. This inner strength changes your very nature. Surviving a difficult time makes you a better man, one equipped for the additional trials life is sure to bring along. That in itself gives you confidence for the days ahead.

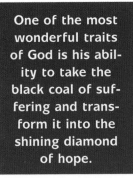

One of the most wonderful traits of God is his ability to take the black coal of suffering and transform it into the shining diamond of hope.

Even more important, by sustaining you through a time of pain, God will prove to you that your trust in him is well placed. The end product of suffering with God at your side is a greater hope in him, gained through both seeing how he can strengthen you and experiencing his faithfulness. Best of all, your increased assurance in God applies not just to this life but also to the next, leaving you with joyful anticipation for the future he has promised, a time in which there will be no more suffering.

Invite God into your difficult times and allow him to mold you in the midst of them. Turn this key that releases his power to ultimately bring hope out of pain.

What we see will last only a short time,
but what we cannot see will last forever.

2 Corinthians 4:18 ncv

Optical Illusion

How close does this come to describing your idea of a perfect life: a beautiful wife, beautiful children, a beautiful home on beautiful property, a great-looking car, a cool boat or motorcycle, and smiling back at you in the mirror every morning, a handsome specimen of manhood in attractive clothes? You might dismiss all this as shallow, but it reflects a deep yearning in the heart of every guy. The desire for beauty is a powerful force in a man's life.

You could spend all your days chasing the beauty you see around you, and trying to improve your own appearance. But the world's beauty is fleeting and never really satisfies. The truth is, physical beauty is an illusion. What you really want—what you really need—is genuine beauty, which lasts forever and proves itself true because it emanates from a source of pure goodness and love.

Let your profound desire for beauty drive you to God. His beauty is authentic—and could never be described as skin-deep. It's an incomparable loveliness that's completely intertwined with his character. If you have faith, one day you'll see God face-to-face, and you'll be amazed. In the meantime, ask God to help you see and appreciate eternal beauty in this life. It's a reflection of his splendor, and it's all around. Real, unfading beauty shines from each man and woman in whom God is forming that person's character into the likeness of his own.

> **Physical beauty is an illusion. What you really want—what you really need—is genuine beauty, which lasts forever.**

Determine to spend the rest of your life focusing on the things that have eternal beauty and value, the things that matter most to God. Study the Bible so you'll begin to recognize those things.

The prayer of a person living right with God is something powerful to be reckoned with.

JAMES 5:16 MSG

The Vital Link

If you're like most men, you want your life to matter, to make a difference in the lives of others. That's a potent incentive to live God's way, according to James. On the human level, your influence in this world is limited to where you can go and what you can do and say. But on the spiritual level, you can have an unlimited impact on the world through your prayers, if you live according to God's plan.

Long ago God decided that Jesus, who always did what was right, would act as a middleman between himself and others. That's a great gift to anyone who is less than perfect.

However, having Jesus as an intermediary doesn't let you off the hook in terms of improving your behavior. If you want your prayers to be heard, you must maintain a relationship with him that keeps you moving ever closer to the pure lifestyle that pleases God.

Jesus promised his followers that God would grant them anything they asked for in his name, so many men include the phrase "in Jesus' name" in their prayers. If you do, reflect on what this phrase means to you. Is it simply a way to wrap up your prayers when you're finished?

> You can have an unlimited impact on the world through your prayers, if you live according to God's plan.

Are you using it as a magical phrase to ensure that your wishes come true? Determine never to use these words lightly, but to back them up with a wholesome lifestyle that demonstrates your connection to Jesus. That's what vitalizes prayer.

～∭◯

Are you living right with God through a relationship with Jesus? If so, pray confidently and expectantly, as a favored son making a request of a Father who is very pleased with him.

My true disciples produce much fruit. This brings great glory to my Father.

JOHN 15:8 NLT

Measure of Productivity

A disciple is much like an apprentice, a young man who attaches himself to a master craftsman to develop knowledge and skill. The apprentice spends his days at his master's side, listening to him, watching him work, and striving to emulate him. The outcome of this unique bond is twofold: over time, the apprentice becomes more and more like his master, and his handiwork begins to take on the same quality.

The greatest Master of all, Jesus, offers all men a wonderful promise. He doesn't say you *must* generate excellent results in order to join him, but rather guarantees that by affixing yourself to him as his apprentice, you *will*. He himself empowers you to grow and achieve. Being connected to God enables you to perform in the same way that plugging a personal computer into an electrical outlet brings it to life and allows it to be used to accomplish incredible things.

Using a different analogy, one that men from any time period would understand, Jesus described himself as a grapevine and his followers as branches. Just as a branch of a grapevine must be attached to the main vine to bear fruit, you must have an intimate relationship with Jesus to

Being connected to God enables you to perform in the same way that plugging a personal computer into an electrical outlet brings it to life.

show results that please God. It's Jesus' life flowing through you that allows you to produce growth in your character and an impact on others' lives. That's the outcome God seeks.

Connect with God, and stay connected, by inviting him to be your Master and recommitting yourself to him each day. He desires that attachment with you but always gives you the freedom to choose.

The prayer of faith will save the sick, and the Lord will raise him up.

James 5:15 NKJV

Primary Physician

Faith is not some vague, nebulous thing; it's simply an investment of trust. When a man pays health insurance premiums, or allows them to be deducted from his paycheck, he's putting his trust in the insurance company, counting on it to pay for medical care. Likewise, when he goes to the hospital, he's placing his confidence in the skill of doctors and the effectiveness of medicine, relying on them to cure him.

Your faith—in terms of healing—may begin here. It may end here too, or perhaps in addition to your trust in the healthcare system, you have some hope that God will also help heal you. God invites you to make him your primary physician. He encourages you to invest your highest trust in him, not abandoning the healthcare system but going to him first and asking him to make you well. Prayer that expresses this kind of faith is the most essential part of the healing process, and should precede everything else.

God has an advantage over every other healthcare provider: only he can heal a man forever.

When you are sick or injured, put your trust in God. He may restore you directly—he certainly has the power to do so. Or he may guide you to the right doctor and the best treatment and use them to heal you. God will always respond to your prayers; Jesus said that even if a man who believes in him dies, he will still live. God has an advantage over every other healthcare provider: only he can heal a man forever.

Select God as your primary physician. Trust him for healing whenever you or your loved ones are sick or injured, and ask him to guide you in determining what to do about medical treatment.

It is better to be patient than powerful; it is better to have self-control than to conquer a city.

PROVERBS 16:32 NLT

Ruling the Realm

If a man's home is his castle, how should he deal with the peasants who reside there with him? Whether it's living in a college dorm with other guys, staying in an apartment with a roommate, or abiding in your own house with a wife and kids, you'll often have to share your living space with others. Rubbing shoulders with the commoners every day can cause a great deal of friction, unless you take the Bible's advice and decide to be a little more forbearing than the average monarch.

The self-control needed to exercise patience with other people is different from the self-control it takes to manage

anger. Patience is the all-important art of not becoming angry in the first place. It's about slowing down your response time, choosing not to make anger your knee-jerk reaction to every incident. This requires some will power, because it means resisting the natural inclination to get mad whenever someone steps on your toes. How do you do that? Ultimately, by relinquishing your "rights" as the master of your domain and counting yourself among the ordinary folk.

> **Patience, like wisdom, is a gift from God—and they go hand in hand.**

Patience, like wisdom, is a gift from God—and they go hand in hand. Understanding that God values other people's feelings just as much as he values yours will help you to cut your former royal subjects a little slack. Also, God can give you insight into others' points of view, enabling you to empathize with their perspectives and find ways to resolve conflict peacefully and without anger.

Ruling your realm with an iron fist may help you get your way, but it causes division in your relationships. Begin dealing with others patiently; it will bring harmony to your dwelling place.

IMPORTANT
BIBLE VERSES
FOR WOMEN

I will meditate on
Your precepts, and
contemplate Your ways.
I will delight myself in
Your statutes; I will not
forget Your word.

PSALM 119:15–16 NKJV

Be still, and know that I am God; I will be exalted among the nations, I will be exalted in the earth!

PSALM 46:10 NKJV

Quiet amid Chaos

Three words can aptly describe the average woman today: *busy, busy, busy*. She hurries from one project or need to another, taking care of others and balancing demands. Studies show that not only is the average woman busy from the time she gets up to the time she goes to bed, but she also is reducing her sleep time because she has too much to do.

It is tough for many women to slow down for anything—even God. This not only affects a woman's physical life, but also her spiritual life. It is important for women to be still and know God for a couple of reasons. In taking time to be with God, a woman builds her relationship with him. As she focuses on God, she remembers how vast God is. She thinks about

> **It is important for women to be still and know God for a couple of reasons.**

God knowing everything, being everywhere, and being the focus of the universe. That puts her life into perspective as she sees the big picture of God and takes the focus off her own limited world. Perhaps most important, when a woman is still, she is refreshed spiritually and gains a new sense of how important she is to God. As a woman is still before God, she hears his voice—his loving, supportive, reassuring voice.

Slow down. Avoid being so busy with the necessities of life that you forget to nourish your soul. Take time to be still in God's vastness. Somehow everything important will get done, and you'll find fresh rest for your life.

"I say this because I know what I am planning for you," says the LORD. "I have good plans for you, not plans to hurt you. I will give you hope and a good future."

JEREMIAH 29:11 NCV

Showers of Hope and a Sunshiny Future

When it comes to surprise parties, it's sometimes hard to figure out who enjoys the party most—the person being honored or the person doing the planning. Scheming good things for other people can be a blast. God shares the enjoyment of planning good things for people who love him.

Some people interpret Jeremiah 29:11 to mean that when a person loves God, everything in her life will be perfect. That's not necessarily true. Yes, in this verse, God promised the Israelites a great future. But before all the

wonderful things happened, God knew the Israelites would be enslaved by the Babylonians for seventy years. He also knew that at the end, he would return them to their homeland and build a new nation committed to him and to his work.

Many Israelites probably wondered if their servitude would ever end. They worried that they'd die forgotten and enslaved. God assured them that he had a plan for their lives. He would carry out that design day by day. In fact, this strategy was so wonderful that every person who heard it could have hope and sense that the future would be different, better, and even beautiful.

> **God shares the enjoyment of planning good things for people who love him.**

In the Bible, God repeatedly shows care and a great love for his people. He knows each person and has mapped out a plan to grant that person ultimate joy in life and a sense of expectation about the future.

God has a plan for you, for your loved ones, for everyone who loves him. He may lead you through grim times occasionally, but he has a great future full of happiness for everyone who relies on him.

Have I not commanded you? Be strong and of good courage; do not be afraid, nor be dismayed, for the LORD your God is with you wherever you go.

JOSHUA 1:9 NKJV

The God Who Is with You

Joshua must have felt overwhelmed. Moses had died and left him in charge. Moses had led the Israelites out of slavery in Egypt, and Joshua was to lead them into the land they'd been seeking for forty years. Joshua commanded an unruly group of vagabond families, and one of the first tasks on the agenda called for them to fight their way into the land God had promised. Joshua probably thought he couldn't do it, but God gave him reassurance.

When you face seemingly endless household tasks or unruly children or a stress-filled schedule and no time, perhaps you relate to Joshua. You are expected to take hold of the promised land of living faithfully for God in an unfaithful world. You look at your schedule and the amount of work to be done, and you cry, "I can't do this."

God offers you the same reassurance he gave Joshua. You can be strong and courageous. You can be confident and worry-free. You can rest in the understanding that God will give you what you need. When you feel overwhelmed, know that God is with you every step of the way—every step as

You can rest in the understanding that God will give you what you need.

you work in your home, as you run errands, as you care for others. God walks with you and infuses you with strength, courage, and confidence.

When you don't have power, God will empower you. When you don't have the strength, let God step in and give you the strength. Let him work in you and through you. He's willing to—every step of the way.

Mary brought in a pint of very expensive perfume made from pure nard. She poured the perfume on Jesus' feet, and then she wiped his feet with her hair. And the sweet smell from the perfume filled the whole house.

JOHN 12:3 NCV

The Sweet Scent of Worship

Imagine that you're at a home Bible study. All of a sudden, a classy, if not wealthy, woman drops to her knees and washes the Bible study leader's feet with Clive Christian #1, one of the world's most expensive perfumes.

That act would stay in your memory and be a conversation topic for a long time. And that's the reaction people had when Mary anointed Jesus' feet. Actually, several shocking things occurred. The woman's expensive perfume was probably a treasure she'd hoarded. In a culture where women generally acted discreetly around men, she made a spectacle of herself. And in her culture, the foot was considered a rude, nearly unmentionable part of the body. But Mary not only poured her expensive perfume on Jesus' feet, she also used her hair—considered a woman's glory—to wipe his feet.

Why did Mary act in such an unorthodox manner? She wanted to give Jesus her best possession and the most honored part of herself. She wanted to worship him, even though it meant sacrifice.

Real power comes through worship. Through worship, you give God honor. And just as Mary's perfume was a sweet fragrance wafting in the air, your worship is a delectable fragrance to God. By her actions, Mary showed the truest and greatest gift any woman can offer

Real power comes through worship. Through worship, you give God honor.

God: worship. Mary's actions sprang from heart, and John 12:3 is a message of God's greatest desire and a woman's greatest gift to him in one stop.

Joyous and sacrificial worship comes in many forms. Whatever your gift, give it to God, and let the fragrance of worship refresh him and strengthen your heart.

We know that all things work together for good to those who love God, to those who are the called according to His purpose.

ROMANS 8:28 NKJV

All Things

Kim always felt the worst thing that could ever happen was for a person to lose his or her job. So when her boss told her that her position was being eliminated because of budget cuts, she was shocked. She had three months left to find another job, and the company had no openings at her management level. "Actually, losing my job was the best thing that ever happened to me," Kim says today. "It forced me to try to start my own business. And thanks to that, I can work from home and be there for my kids."

Whenever unfortunate events or even tragedies happen, you hear people murmur, "Well, they say everything happens for the best." Often these folks don't realize they're quoting a scriptural promise found in Romans 8:28. God is aware of every situation you encounter, and he can fit it all into the master plan for your life.

> God is aware of every situation you encounter, and he can fit it all into the master plan for your life.

That doesn't mean everything that happens to you will be good. You live in a world where problems and difficulties happen daily, where bad things strike without notice, to all people. But no matter what happens in your life, God promises he will use it—even the tragedies—for some redeeming purpose. He is Lord in your life, during the good days and even in the bad moments.

Today, no matter what life throws at you, rest in the promise and the hope that God can use anything, good or bad, to create the beautiful tapestry of your life.

Ruth said: "Entreat me not to leave you, or to turn back from following after you; for wherever you go, I will go; and wherever you lodge, I will lodge; your people shall be my people, and your God, my God."

RUTH 1:16 NKJV

Loyalty Is a Choice

One of life's most joyous elements is relationships. All people are relational, building intimacy and love with relatives, friends, and acquaintances. Undoubtedly, you have many important and close contacts in your life that you value and cherish. You want to build and sustain close relationships. You want to make them even more intimate, and more compelling.

This most important passage from the Bible shows Ruth relating to her mother-in-law, Naomi. With both of their lives devastated by death and disease, they ended up widows in a foreign land. When Naomi told Ruth to return to her people, Ruth resisted. Her loyalty to Naomi was so intense that she wanted to go with Naomi back to her homeland.

Ruth said she would stay with Naomi, live where she lived, accept Naomi's people as her own, and worship the same God Naomi worshiped.

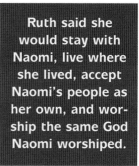

> Ruth said she would stay with Naomi, live where she lived, accept Naomi's people as her own, and worship the same God Naomi worshiped.

What drove Ruth to this commitment? Scholars might answer many ways—love, a sense of moral right, a realization that without Naomi she had nothing—but one answer is paramount: Ruth chose to remain loyal to Naomi. She could have gone back to her people, no questions asked. But she chose to love, follow, and live with Naomi.

Ruth's decision to stay with Naomi demonstrates the essence of commitment to another person: it is a choice you make every day.

Take a look at the choices you make in your relationships. Work at being loyal, loving, giving, honest, forthright, and vulnerable. Loyalty will seal your relationships and make you one who is trusted and loved.

$\mathbb{I}$ will bless her, and indeed I will give you a son by her. Then I will bless her, and she shall be a mother of nations; kings of peoples will come from her.

GENESIS 17:16 NASB

God's Special Blessing

Most women sooner or later will seek some special blessing from God. They usually ask for something they really want. Instead of asking God for the blessing you desire, give God the opportunity to bless you the way he wants to. It is possible that God has a blessing for you that you could never imagine, but which, when granted, will make your life more beautiful and joyous than ever before.

At ninety years old, Sarah, Abraham's wife, had never had children. Probably in her earlier years, Sarah had prayed for a child. But as time wore her down and age wore her out, she probably gave up on hoping for that blessing. Even though when Abraham was seventy-five God had promised him a son (when Sarah was sixty-five), nothing happened for years. Finally, Sarah suggested that Abraham have a child with her maidservant, Hagar.

Instead of asking God for the blessing you desire, give God the opportunity to bless you the way he wants to.

Sarah and Abraham were trying to fulfill God's promise through human means, and the culture in that day approved this method of producing an heir.

Ultimately, though, God rejected Hagar's son, Ishmael, and continued to promise Abraham that he'd have his own son through Sarah. The unexpected blessing came because Sarah wanted a child. God offered a son. Abraham wanted an heir. God made him the father of nations. God's personal blessing was far greater than the blessing Sarah sought.

Your blessing may not be a longed-for son. But if like Sarah you look to the Lord, his blessing will come. And it will bless you in the unique way only the God of grace can imagine.

Mary said, "I am the servant of the Lord. Let this happen to me as you say!" Then the angel went away.

LUKE 1:38 NCV

Mary, the Lord's Servant

Mary was probably only fourteen or fifteen years old when she learned that she was to become the mother of Jesus. She was years ahead of many women—and men, too—when it came to trusting God. Imagine how she must have felt. The man of her dreams had finally proposed. She was eagerly planning for the big wedding and happily-ever-after. Then God asked her to do something unbelievably difficult.

Mary was intelligent. As the angel explained the scenario, Mary immediately understood what this meant in light of the big picture. Pregnancy outside marriage meant she would be disgraced, possibly even stoned. Her family would suffer from that scorn; perhaps they would disbelieve her or turn on her. By placing her reputation in God's hands, Mary was risking the loss of the man she loved and the glorious future that was starting to unfold in her life. If she decided to trust God, her whole life might fall about her in ruins. But Mary was a woman of faith and trust. No negotiations. No whining. No pleading for a guarantee that her life would come out all right in the end. She just asked one technical question, "How can this impossible

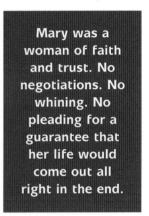

Mary was a woman of faith and trust. No negotiations. No whining. No pleading for a guarantee that her life would come out all right in the end.

thing happen?" And then she responded, "I am the Lord's servant. May it be unto me as you have said."

Mary's response to God as recorded in Luke 1:38 is an excellent model for women to emulate. God would like the same faithful and trusting response from you.

God may ask you to do things that will seem impossible. But as you trust and follow Mary's example, "May it be unto me," and you'll find that he walks with you through the impossible situations.

There is therefore now no condemnation to those who are in Christ Jesus, who do not walk according to the flesh, but according to the Spirit.

ROMANS 8:1 NKJV

Black Clouds Begone

These days you don't have to be in court to watch the procedures. Through cable, television, movies, and the media, you can watch cases from your own home. At the end of the trial you'll see the defendant stand as the verdict is read. Often it is "Guilty as charged." The next stage is for the judge to give the sentence. After the judge pronounces the sentence—"Death by lethal injection," "Life imprisonment"—the accused, perhaps wrestling with self-hatred and inner recriminations, is led out of the courtroom.

No one looks forward to being judged in a court of law. Similarly, no person relishes the idea of standing before God and having his errors read. Guilt is a horrible thing. It makes you feel low, small, hated, and broken.

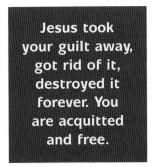

Romans 8:1 speaks volumes of hope to every woman who feels the cringe and crush of guilt and judgment. Even though you may not be accused in a court of law, guilt can still pronounce a judgment on your life and make you feel miserable for hours, months, years. There is a great truth about guilt. Its black cloud no longer hovers over your head. No one in heaven accuses you. Jesus took your guilt away, got rid of it, destroyed it forever. You are acquitted and free. Your thoughts may accuse, but they are lies. Jesus freed you from guilt and self-hatred and gives you new thoughts and joys.

Jesus took your guilt away, got rid of it, destroyed it forever. You are acquitted and free.

Do you want real freedom from guilt? Because of Jesus' death on the cross, you are no longer guilty. You are new, clean, and beautiful in his eyes. He doesn't judge you, so don't judge yourself. You are free to live in joy and peace.

Always be willing to listen and slow to speak. Do not become angry easily, because anger will not help you live the right kind of life God wants.

JAMES 1:19–20 NCV

Breaking Out of an Angry Episode

Every woman has felt anger—sometimes deep anger—over bad treatment, disobedient children, an insensitive husband. What might dispel the anger you feel? What truth can you turn to that will eliminate the bitterness in your soul?

James gave you this most important verse about anger. He offered three pertinent guidelines to anyone who feels the sting of inner anger. First, be willing to listen. Listening gives the person you're angry with a chance to make a defense, or at least to explain his or her actions. But if you jump all over him before you've given him a hearing, how will you know if your anger is justified? Listen. Perhaps a solution will be apparent, or perhaps you will find that a mis-communication has occurred. If you are willing to listen to the other person, he or she will be more likely to listen to your perspective.

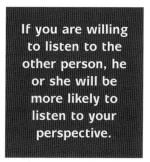

If you are willing to listen to the other person, he or she will be more likely to listen to your perspective.

Second, be "slow to speak." James meant for you to think, to meditate, to look at the situation from all angles. Don't jump to conclusions and berate your opponent. Consider the situation in depth before you respond. Third, remain "slow to anger." Okay, you've listened, thought it all through, but you're still angry. What is the answer? Calm yourself. Dampen the anger. Don't speak harshly. Seek self-control with the help of God's Spirit.

—※—

If you follow James's practical steps when you feel angry, you will never say things you regret or cause more pain because of your reaction.

Since God has shown us great mercy, I beg you to offer your lives as a living sacrifice to him. Your offering must be only for God and pleasing to him, which is the spiritual way for you to worship.

ROMANS 12:1 NCV

Your Greatest Sacrifice

An old story pictures a young, recently converted woman waking up in the morning. As her eyes open and her mind clears, she repeats a little ceremony she does every morning. Without getting out of bed, she prays: "This bed is the altar; I am the sacrifice. I give my life to you this day, O God, all of today. Use me as you wish. I am your servant." With those words, she gets up, dresses, and goes into her day ready to serve God and to respond when she hears his voice in her heart.

As a servant of God, think of yourself as a sacrifice to him. Paul wrote to the Roman believers to encourage them to give themselves to God in this way. Personal sacrifice is a voluntary thing; God doesn't demand it from you. Paul merely encouraged the Romans to take this step, and his words encour-

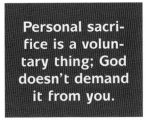

Personal sacrifice is a voluntary thing; God doesn't demand it from you.

age you to do the same—every day, if necessary. This is the best way to worship God, by giving yourself to him.

You make this sacrifice through a simple choice: choose to tell God you want him to use you for his purposes. Ask him to work in your life, to lead you, and to empower you. You may not notice the difference immediately, but as you live for him day by day you will see it. New energy and enthusiasm will flood your heart. A great desire to get involved in his work in the world will grip you.

Give yourself up to God's leading, will, and purpose. This is the truest and surest route to the blessings he plans to give you in this life.

God is Spirit, and those who worship Him must worship in spirit and truth.

JOHN 4:24 NKJV

True Worship

A young woman sways to praise music in a large church sanctuary. In the front row, a middle-aged woman gets out of her seat, turns, and kneels in the pew with her head in her hands to pray. In the middle of the sanctuary, another woman sits, her eyes open, her lips moving, but with no words coming out.

Clearly, all three women could be worshiping God in ways that please God. What they show is that it isn't the outward position—kneeling, standing, sitting, dancing—or the exuberance of the expression. Rather the heart connection is what counts.

Worship is the highest expression of human love and devotion to God. Jesus' words in John 4:24 reveal that worship most truly occurs when your spirit connects with God's Spirit, when the real you meets the real him and honors him for his love, grace and sacrifice. You can do that in any position, in any place, at any time, and with any attitude. Most people occasionally feel that their worship is little more than going through motions. Ask God to work in you his real, Spirit-to-spirit worship. Ask the Spirit of God to guide you. As you grow and learn, worship will become a blessed reality and a part of your life that you could never forget, overlook, or skip.

Worship is the highest expression of human love and devotion to God.

Real, intimate worship is worth the effort to develop in your life.

The LORD is constantly watching everyone, and he gives strength to those who faithfully obey him.

2 CHRONICLES 16:9 CEV

The Eye in the Sky

Some cities are implementing a new program at traffic lights. Cameras at intersections take pictures of the license plates of cars running red lights. Then the car owners automatically get tickets in the mail. The message from the police force is clear: "We're watching you." The same thing is true in many department and grocery stores—surveillance cameras keep an electronic eye on customers.

As powerful as electronic eyes are, they're nothing compared with God. If you were raised in church, you probably

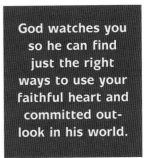

know a few songs about God's eyes being on you. It would be easy to get into the frame of mind that God is like a traffic cop or surveillance camera—just waiting to catch you being bad. Entertainer Mark Lowry counters this attitude. He tells his audiences that God doesn't watch his people to see if he can catch them doing wrong; he watches because he is in love with his people. "God's eyes are constantly on you," Lowry exclaims. "He can't take his eyes off you because he loves you so much."

> God watches you so he can find just the right ways to use your faithful heart and committed outlook in his world.

God is watching. But not to condemn. God's eyes go throughout the world, and he looks for those with character and faithfulness. God watches you so he can find just the right ways to use your faithful heart and committed outlook in his world. He could do the job alone, but he wants to employ you to help.

God's eyes are watching you today. As he sees you obeying him, he'll continue to fill your life with his strength, power, and love.

A gentle answer turns away wrath, but a harsh word stirs up anger.

PROVERBS 15:1 NASB

The Spiral Stopper

Disagreements often go like this: "Why didn't you take the trash out?" "Oh, I forgot." "You forget everything." "No, I don't. I remembered—" "No, you're the most forgetful person I ever met." "You're just mean." "Oh, you want to see mean?" And on and on it goes.

Arguments often start over minor issues—someone forgot to do what he promised, or someone forgot to say she'd be a little late, or someone did or didn't do something else—but these issues can escalate from the inconsequential into accusations, put-downs, and painful words that both parties remember long and regret at their leisure. There is a way to break that spiral and to keep an argument from becoming nasty.

Proverbs 15:1 ranks high among the all-time great solutions for women who can't seem to end the quarrel spiral. The solution is to answer gently, even if it is easier to speak defensively. A gentle answer can bring an argument to an abrupt halt. Instead of shooting a comeback that stings, say something gentle; perhaps even agree with the

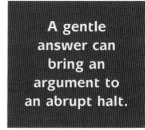

A gentle answer can bring an argument to an abrupt halt.

other person. "I'm sorry." "I'll try to do better." "Please forgive me." Such mild answers defuse an argument and bring it to a halt. Even if your antagonist responds with something like "You always say that," keep speaking those easygoing sentences. Stifle a mean comeback. Eventually this tactic will work.

The gentle response can cool off a hot situation and turn it into a time to learn, to grow, and to better understand others. A peacemaker always wins God's blessing.

The LORD says, "My thoughts are not like your thoughts. Your ways are not like my ways. Just as the heavens are higher than the earth, so are my ways higher than your ways and my thoughts higher than your thoughts."

ISAIAH 55:8–9 NCV

Who Can Understand God?

Experience is wonderful. Teaching a young teen to drive will remind you of that fact. So will training an inexperienced new employee.

Experience is a terrific tool. But no matter how much experience, knowledge, and understanding you have about life, you, and all humans, still fall way short of God. He is on a plane higher than mortals can even fathom. His thoughts

aren't the same as yours. Sometimes people get caught in the trap of thinking that God is like them—only smarter. But a couple of verses in Isaiah say that the best of human brains aren't even on the same playing field as God. God isn't just smarter; his thinking is beyond anything humans are capable of. If women are mentally from Venus

> **God promises to come through in your life in a way that will work for you and satisfy you.**

and men are mentally from Mars, well, then God is from heaven.

For you as a woman, this means that when your path appears blocked, God sees a way. When you see the finite world around you and the challenges it brings, God sees beyond them. God sees far beyond your world. God is totally superior to humans. You can trust God, and you can turn to him when you need someone bigger, someone whose knowledge is all-encompassing. God promises to come through in your life in a way that will work for you and satisfy you.

When you don't know what decision to make, when you feel stymied or oppressed, remember God. He can carve a path through that problem.

God, with his mercy, gave us this work
to do, so we don't give up.

2 CORINTHIANS 4:1 NCV

The Joys
of Service

Go to your local elementary school on the day of a holiday party to check out the power of volunteerism in action. Chances are that you'll find the halls swarming with men and women who want to help. Or notice all the people behind the scenes at a community fund-raiser. Watch their faces, and you'll probably notice that they're having a great time.

Most women have areas of service in their lives. Whether it's at church or in the community, women tend to enjoy using their talents and skills to support events and organizations. When women get involved, things happen.

Women often have these opportunities to help others not because of chance but because God has given the situations to them. God has a purpose and a plan for your life. Sometimes those areas are part of that. Through serving, you can have an impact on the lives of men, children, and other women. Your commitment and kindness might be an example to someone else of how kind

When women get involved, things happen.

and committed God is. Your willingness to help might show someone how God can help him or her. Seeing you using your abilities might encourage others to give their time and talent too.

Your involvement doesn't just benefit others. God gives you these areas to help through his mercy. You're not only doing good things for others, but you also reap profit. As you help others, you'll find that God rewards you in interesting, intriguing, and fun ways.

⁓

The next time you receive an opportunity to serve, enjoy it. Remember that it might be something God has placed in your life to improve your life and the lives of those around you.

Do not be conformed to this world, but be transformed by the renewing of your mind, that you may prove what is that good and acceptable and perfect will of God.

ROMANS 12:2 NKJV

Transformed

"I want to be a better person." "I wish I wouldn't react that way all the time." "I can't stop myself. It just happens, and then I feel wretched." Most women have said such words and want desperately to be different than they are. Bad habits, stress reactions, and harsh responses make women feel guilty. But you can overcome such character traits.

God can make you a new and different person, and he can tame that tiger in your soul. Notice what Paul said in his

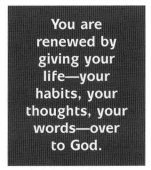

letter to the Romans. He said you shouldn't be conformed to or in harmony with the world. Rather, you should be "transformed by the renewing of your mind." That "renewing" is the crucial idea here. You are renewed by giving your life—your habits, your thoughts, your words—over to God. You commit yourself to listening to him and seeking what he wants for you. Gradually, day by day, God's Spirit works in your heart to change you.

> You are renewed by giving your life—your habits, your thoughts, your words—over to God.

A woman who lived in an arid climate wanted to grow grass in her yard. But it rained rarely. She planted the seeds, but they never grew, except in one place. The little patch of ground outside her kitchen window grew lush grass. What was the difference? Every day, she doused that part of her yard with the dishwater.

Dousing your mind with Bible knowledge, talking to God, and listening for his voice will transform you. Like that little patch of grass, you will grow a renewed mind that loves the good and does right.

Is anything too hard for the LORD? No! I will return to you at the right time a year from now, and Sarah will have a son.

GENESIS 18:14 NCV

Nothing Too Hard for God

The average woman would be alarmed if angels showed up at her door and told her that even though she's long past childbearing years, she is going to have a baby. Sarah laughed. It wasn't that she didn't want to have a child. For most of her ninety or so years she'd tried to get pregnant. And this wasn't the first time God had sent the message that she was to become a mother. He'd said that before and nothing happened. So Sarah had tried to "help" God out by encouraging her servant girl to have a child with her husband, Abraham — a child she planned to raise. But Sarah's schemes to help fulfill God's promise ended up in a mess.

Don't give up on God. His timing is not the same as yours.

After years had passed, God reminded Sarah and Abraham of his promise. Sarah's laughter indicated that she had given up on ever holding that baby. But the angels reminded her, "Is anything too hard for the LORD?"

Perhaps you believe that God promised you something, but you haven't seen the promise fulfilled. When that happens, it's tempting to try to finagle people and situations to make the desired results happen. And after disappointment, it's tempting to just give up on God. Don't give up on God. Keep your hope in him. His timing is not the same as yours.

What God promises, he will do. Put your faith into high gear and wait for him to act when everything is just right. Remember, nothing is impossible for God.

Do not be drunk with wine, which will ruin you, but be filled with the Spirit.

EPHESIANS 5:18 NCV

The Friend Who Is Always Beside You

Many people who read the Bible stumble when they come across the command to be filled with the Spirit. Actually, being filled with the Spirit is a relatively simple concept, and it's one of the most exciting promises in the Bible. *Filled* means "to be led, controlled, empowered" by the Spirit of God. Becoming filled with the Spirit is not dif-ficult—you don't have to go through any long processes. You become filled with the Spirit in your life simply by turn-ing over your motivations and concerns to God. Through the Spirit who lives in you—a bit of a mystical concept, but a reality to those who invite him to take charge of their lives—you find that God gives you resources day by day to live as he wants you to. At times, you may be sitting in a doctor's office, in church, or at a meeting, and the Spirit will speak to you. The Spirit's voice might direct you in many areas—often with small

The filling of the Spirit is like having a friend right inside your mind and heart.

details. He might suggest, *Make yourself a note to write a letter of encouragement to this person*. Or he may draw your attention to a certain person. *Go chat with that one. She looks like she needs to talk to someone*.

The filling of the Spirit is like having a friend right inside your mind and heart. He can speak, lead, encourage, or empower you at any time. At times, you won't even be aware that he is there because his gentle touch is so subtle.

Let the Spirit lead, guide, empower, and enfold you. Let him take full rein in your life. If you do, you will see God work through you in awesome ways.

Because you have these blessings, do your best to add these things to your lives: to your faith, add goodness; and to your goodness, add knowledge.

2 Peter 1:5 ncv

Working on Your Masterpiece

In 1932, a carpenter began to use his off-season to make children's toys. Pretty soon, the toys were selling so well that he dropped the carpentry business. One of his creations is one of America's all-time favorite toys—something you probably played with when you were a child: LEGO construction toys. The object of LEGO is that you attach plastic bricks to other plastic bricks and keep adding more bricks to the previously laid bricks until you build a wonderful masterpiece.

What a good analogy of a woman's spiritual life. As a woman strives to be closer to God, and to be more like him, she is building. Her foundation is having a relationship with God as she places her faith in him. On top of her faith, a woman builds goodness—she develops qualities such as decency, morality, and kindness. To make her faith more well-rounded and effective,

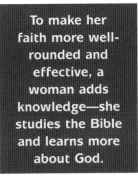

To make her faith more well-rounded and effective, a woman adds knowledge—she studies the Bible and learns more about God.

a woman adds knowledge—she studies the Bible and learns more about God.

Building faith doesn't come automatically, so a person has to work at it sometimes. You can have fun as you look for ways to be examples of God's goodness here on earth. And you can enjoy learning more about God and his grace and his love for people. It might even be as rewarding and enjoyable as, well, as building something with LEGO bricks.

As you move through your life today, look for ways to build your faith. Have your own spiritual treasure hunt, looking for those blocks that will make you stronger and more beautiful than ever.

183

These are the ways of the world: wanting to please our sinful selves, wanting the sinful things we see, and being too proud of what we have. None of these come from the Father, but all of them come from the world. The world and everything that people want in it are passing away, but the person who does what God wants lives forever.

1 JOHN 2:16–17 NCV

The Gotta-Have-It Test

At some time in your life, you've probably been asked a variation of this question: "If your house was on fire and you had three minutes to grab anything, what would you save?"

Perhaps every woman should ask herself that question periodically. It helps you center on what is really important in your life—what *you* know is truly a priority. Think about it now. What would you grab on your way out? Your purse? Your family pictures? Your new name-brand gadget? Every day plenty of people and companies bombard you with their ideas of what's important in your life. They'll tell you that you have to have a great car to show how powerful you are and to keep you comfortable. You have to have certain clothes so you can look great, and better yet, get rid of the imperfections you've always hated in your body—those things that make you different—

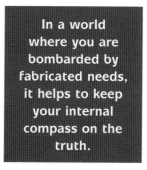

In a world where you are bombarded by fabricated needs, it helps to keep your internal compass on the truth.

through simple surgical enhancements. Buy a fabulous home so you can impress the friends you don't have time to have over. You know the advertising and marketing routines.

In a world where you are bombarded by fabricated needs, it helps to keep your internal compass on the truth. Periodically assess your life and discern what's really valued in your life. And remember to invest in what you can take with you to heaven.

If your life ended tomorrow, think about what you'd take with you and what intangibles you would leave behind. Keep your life in perspective.

Brothers and sisters, do not be surprised when the people of the world hate you.

1 JOHN 3:13 NCV

Popularity Contest?

When Joy became a manager, she received lots of advice from other managers. She valued all of it, but she says the best advice she received was this: "Managing is not a popularity contest." She worked in a new business, where many young up-and-comers were employed. Getting them in line and keeping them focused took discipline and sometimes a stern word or two. Many times in life you simply have to say or do things whether other people approve or not. Your responsibility supersedes your congeniality.

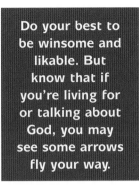

Maybe you have faced this with your faith and morals. When you are striving to live for God, others may not understand that. They may not understand why you feel some attitudes and actions are wrong and why you support other ones. The important thing is to focus on the reality of living for God in a world where he isn't a priority. It is your responsibility and your privilege to live for God despite social impediments or major differences of opinion.

> Do your best to be winsome and likable. But know that if you're living for or talking about God, you may see some arrows fly your way.

Of course, that doesn't give you a license to be abrasive. Do your best to be winsome and likable. Friendliness is a good thing. But know that if you're living for or talking about God, you may see some arrows fly your way. If so, then do what you have to do.

Keep living for God. If someone doesn't understand, just keep following what you believe—and ask God to open the other person's eyes.

Do all things without complaining and disputing.

PHILIPPIANS 2:14 NKJV

The Attitude Cleaner

Glenda took on a new attitude when she became a Christian. Instead of complaining about others as she used to do, she often said, "God isn't through with them yet." When before she might have run off into a stream of curses or sarcastic comments about someone's mistake, she now said things like "I guess God had a different idea about that one." And when things simply didn't go her way, she took the positive view and said, "Thanks, God. You're giving me something to think about" or "I hadn't thought about that, God."

Not everyone can have such an attitude overnight, but Philippians 2:14 points out the style of life God's followers should have: no grumbling, complaining, or put-downs. Instead, find words of praise, thanks, affirmation, and encouragement.

Some people say it is easier said than done, but the starting point is simply refusing to complain or criticize when things go wrong. Fill your mind with good thoughts, healthy thinking, and words that refresh. Memorize Scriptures

Fill your mind with good thoughts, healthy thinking, and words that refresh.

that can drive out the grumbling. Turn yourself into the one who always has something good to say, rather than be someone who always grumbles or makes snide comments. God will help you. Ask God to get involved with your attitude, and you'll find him reminding you when such words try to get out of your mouth.

Someone once said, "If you don't have anything good to say, don't say anything." Maybe a variation will help: "If you don't have anything good to say, say something good anyway."

With God's power working in us, God can do much, much more than anything we can ask or imagine.

EPHESIANS 3:20 NCV

You Can't Even Imagine It

Jan came home stunned by what she had heard that night. The speaker had challenged his listeners to start thinking big for God. At one point, he quoted the powerful Ephesians 3:20 and said, "If God told you that you could ask him to do anything in this world in the next year, what would you ask for?" Jan didn't know, but she found herself thinking seriously about it.

She began to think bigger and wider than she'd ever thought before. The news about the tsunami in Southeast

Asia had mobilized the world, and that was pretty big. But then she thought: *What about an outpouring of God's Spirit on those people? How about the involvement of many others in helping them?*

She began praying about that and other things. God soon led her to put wings to her prayers, and she got involved in a missions effort to Cambodia. She flew halfway around the world and helped those poor people start a fishing industry. It was miraculous. Many Cambodians became believers in

God wants you to try to imagine greater things for him to do than ever before.

Jesus, and fast friendships were formed that Jan knew would last forever.

Don't let anyone tell you that thinking big is not biblical. God wants you to try to imagine greater things for him to do than ever before. Lay them at his feet. Make them your heart's prayer.

When God does big things in the world, it is because his followers have prayed for big things to happen. Get involved. Pray big, and God will do big—more than you can think or imagine.

$\mathbb{I}$ correct and punish those whom I love. So be eager to do right, and change your hearts and lives.

REVELATION 3:19 NCV

When God Gives You a Time-Out

Anyone who has worked with small children is familiar with time-outs. When a child refuses to obey, smacks another tot, or infringes on other rules, he or she may be escorted to a chair for the time-out—often one minute per age. This gentle discipline system is designed to make kids stop, think about what they're doing, and make better choices. After the time-out is over, the child is free to rejoin the excitement.

As children grow up, their parents stop disciplining them, but even grownups sometimes still feel God's hand of correction. Different people respond in various manners when they face God's discipline. Some argue and refuse to admit they did anything wrong, or they put the blame on someone else. Others not only agree with God that they've done something wrong, but they also use the opportunity to beat themselves up emotionally—to go into a depression and think of how horrible

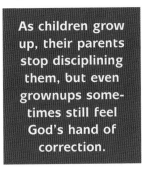

As children grow up, their parents stop disciplining them, but even grownups some-times still feel God's hand of correction.

they are. They hang on to the fact that they've done some-thing wrong, and feel like a failure.

Like a time-out, God's discipline isn't meant to last for-ever. He doesn't "spiritually spank" people to be cruel or to flaunt his power. Instead, his discipline is designed to catch a person's attention, to show her where she's wrong, and to help her think of the better choices she'll make the next time. Discipline is a sign of God's love—if he didn't love you, he wouldn't care how you act.

—

The next time you feel God's discipline, accept it, ask him to forgive you, and move on. God wants your heart to walk in freedom from guilt.

My God shall supply all your need according to His riches in glory by Christ Jesus.

PHILIPPIANS 4:19 NKJV

All Your Needs

Every woman has her dream. Cheryl's dream was to quit her job and stay home with her young children. She talked with her husband and prayed about it. Through her prayers, Cheryl felt God was approving her desire, so she took the plunge. She figured ways to save enough money to make up for the salary she'd brought in. Frequently she asked God to financially take care of her family. She learned they could survive without her full-time income.

God didn't mysteriously shower Cheryl's family with money. They learned to do without some things. Cheryl feels that God helped her catch tremendous sales. God provided everything Cheryl's family needed. She was even able to start an organization and Web site called Homebodies to help other moms, and she wrote two books to help women achieve their dreams to stay at home.

Philippians 4:19 gives women a wonderful reminder that God will take care of them. Usually this verse is mentioned in a fiscal context as people, like Cheryl, learn that God takes care of them financially. But the verse goes beyond that. It is a reminder that God meets every need in your life. Perhaps you have an emotional need; perhaps you

> God didn't mysteriously shower Cheryl's family with money. They learned to do without some things.

need more patience with those around you. God can meet your needs. Maybe you need encouragement and hope. God can provide it. You might even need a new washing machine. Talk to God about it. God may not provide all of your wants, but he'll meet every necessity.

It is human nature to want to be independent and take care of yourself. But give God a chance. Ask him to meet your needs and look for the obvious and subtle ways he provides.

Samuel replied, "What is more pleasing to the LORD: your burnt offerings and sacrifices or your obedience to his voice? Obedience is far better than sacrifice. Listening to him is much better than offering the fat of rams."

1 SAMUEL 15:22 NLT

Obedience vs. Sacrifice

Imagine that your boss enters your coworker's cubicle and asks her to drop everything and prepare a report for a 3:00 p.m. meeting. She says "sure" and gets busy. She looks for some data and finally finds it in a stack of papers to be filed, and so she files the stack while she's at it. As she does so, she finds two other half-finished reports and decides to quickly finish them. Then printer problems require twenty minutes. Your coworker returns to the 3:00 p.m. report. You take pity on her and help. But it isn't enough. At 3:00 p.m., your boss shows up and the report isn't quite done. "But I worked hard all day," your coworker moans. You know it's true. You feel for your coworker, but you understand your boss's perspective: though your coworker did some good things, she didn't follow the boss's orders.

> Sometimes it's easier for women to sacrifice time, resources, and energy for God instead of just doing what he told them to do.

Saul had the same kind of problem. He was sacrificing to God, and that appears to be a good thing to do. It's good, that is, unless God has told you to do something else. Saul didn't want to follow God's directives, so maybe he thought God would excuse him if he did other good things instead. But it didn't work that way. God wanted obedience.

Sometimes it's easier for women to sacrifice time, resources, and energy for God instead of just doing what he told them to do. No matter how great your sacrifices, God would rather have obedience.

~❦

As you obey God, the work of his kingdom will get done more efficiently and effectively. Sacrifices for God are good—but obeying his Word and directions is more important.

The only temptation that has come to you is that which everyone has. But you can trust God, who will not permit you to be tempted more than you can stand. But when you are tempted, he will also give you a way to escape so that you will be able to stand it.

1 CORINTHIANS 10:13 NCV

The Escape Hatch

In the fourth century, asceticism rose to its highest popularity. Ascetics were people who typically denied themselves the usual comforts of sleep, food, water, bed, and home. They did this, they believed, to avoid temptation. For instance, Saint Ascepsimas wore numerous chains to remind himself of his penchant for temptation. Brother Besarion, a monk, refused sleep, and wouldn't lie down for forty years. Saint Maron lived in a hollow tree trunk, where he was supposedly safe from the influences of the world. There have been stories of ascetics in modern times who self-deny in the belief that to do so will obtain for them a higher spiritual or moral state.

Such measures do little to stop temptation. Instead, the Bible provides a far superior remedy. If one verse in the Bible stands out as a guide for dealing with temptation, 1 Corinthians 10:13 is it. Everyone faces temptation. You can't escape it. When you admit temptation is there and get prayer help, you find that others have faced the same thing. You can claim God's promise that he won't let temptation become so strong that you have to give in. He

You can claim God's promise that he won't let temptation become so strong that you have to give in.

will guide you to an incredible escape hatch. Running and fleeing the temptation, resisting the temptation, or finding something else to do are all good strategies.

You don't have to give in to temptation, but God encourages you to turn to him for help, guidance, and comfort.

The next time temptation taunts you, turn to God and ask him to show you his way of escape. He will, and you'll be free.

Great is our Lord, and mighty in power;
His understanding is infinite.

PSALM 147:5 NKJV

He
Understands

Friends, moms, and God all tend to have something in common: they understand. Think of a person in your life who is a good friend. You have probably spent hours together and shared many experiences. As a result, you understand each other. The more you communicate, the more you understand each other's perspective and understand where the other person is coming from. You may not always agree with your friend's choices, but you probably understand why she made them.

The same may be true if you have children or are around them. If you watch children to figure out what makes them tick, what motivates them, you'll better understand the reasons why they do some of the things they do. For instance, when you

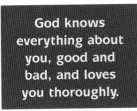

God knows everything about you, good and bad, and loves you thoroughly.

realize your child is afraid of monsters under the bed, you have a little more patience and understanding when he or she doesn't want to sleep in his room alone.

One of the most glorious facts about having a relationship with God is the realization that he understands your deepest desires and hopes. He realizes the temptations you face. He knows how hard you try. God knows everything about you, good and bad, and loves you thoroughly. Because he understands you so well, you can trust him and turn to him at any time.

Never hesitate to turn to God in your joy, or in your challenges. He understands your motivations, your struggles, and your faith.

I have been young, and now am old; yet I have not seen the righteous forsaken, nor his descendants begging bread.

PSALM 37:25 NKJV

Never Forsaken

An Indian woman at a missions conference in Calcutta stood before a large crowd and held up hands with only a few fingers. Because her body was ravaged by leprosy, it was hard for many even to look at her. But her face was radiant. "Thank God," she said. "Thank God for my leprosy. For because of it, I came to know him. I was drawn to him because of my suffering, and I became a believer in him when I realized his love and goodness. From that time, I have never been hungry or thirsty, and I have helped many

others find in him the answer to their deepest needs." She then quoted Psalm 37:25, adding that it had proved true in her life.

God sometimes guides circumstances, whether good or bad, in order to draw you closer to himself. At times you may have a need because he wants you to turn to him for help. When he answers, he will be glorified and your faith will be built up. This verse from the Psalms shows you the powerful truth that God never leaves his children begging. He will always respond to your needs and meet them

> **God sometimes guides circumstances, whether good or bad, in order to draw you closer to himself.**

on his timetable. You can trust that he has allowed that need to exist because he wants you to pray and ask him to meet it.

This verse is central for you because it reminds you that when you're living for God, he is going to see that you are taken care of. He will care for you emotionally and materially, and will care for you and your children.

Take a hard look at your life. You probably have new needs every day. Turn to God and watch him supply, and then you can tell the world how God really does supply everything.

IMPORTANT
BIBLE VERSES
FOR teens

Let no one despise
your youth, but be an
example to the believers
in word, in conduct, in
love, in spirit, in faith,
in purity.

1 TIMOTHY 4:12 NKJV

In the beginning God created the heavens and the earth.

GENESIS 1:1 NKJV

In the Beginning God Thought of You

Don't you wish you could have been there when God created the world? The process of designing the moon, the sun, and the planets must have been incredible. The power and creativity give you just a glimpse of God and all he is capable of. Creating heaven and earth involved science, math, biology, chemistry, and all sorts of other school subjects that humans wouldn't begin to discover until years after the creation event.

Much of creation remains a mystery today. A lot of what God does is just too huge for the human mind to comprehend. The creation of the heavens and the earth is a loud statement from God to you about who he is, how powerful he is, and what his plan is. God used his power to arrange the intimate details of the world you live in. God didn't make just one tree for you; he made hundreds of thousands of species of trees.

> If God can create a star out of nothing, imagine what he can do with your life.

God's power created all you need to live including water, food, and shelter. His abilities go beyond supplying your physical needs, however; he supplies direction for a great life. It is no small thing to create even one star. If God can create a star out of nothing, imagine what he can do with your life. It is comforting to know that even in the beginning God took a personal interest in you and provided exactly what you need to live.

God designed the world with you in mind. Look around and enjoy the details of life that God made for you to enjoy. Look for God in the details around you.

The LORD is good, a stronghold in the day of trouble; and He knows those who trust in Him.

NAHUM 1:7 NKJV

God Protects You

The people of Nineveh had messed up once before, and a hundred years later they were again choosing to live their own way. By indulging their desires, they had removed themselves from the safety and protection of God. Getting your way has a certain appeal in the beginning because it seems to offer freedom, fun, sensuality, and excitement. The appeal, however, is lost once you realize your way may not be as good as God's way for your life. His way for your life includes boundaries, but they are designed to ensure your safety.

Choosing to live according to God's will is like choosing a safe shelter for your life. The Hebrew word for *stronghold* used in Nahum 1:7 is *ma'owz*, which means "a place of safety, protection, refuge." Imagine two houses. One house is more like a castle with a moat, tall solid walls, and thick wooden doors designed to keep anyone inside safe from harm. The other house has standard doors, walls, and windows. Living in God's will is like living in a castle, compared to living in a regular house.

> **God will be there for you when pain, disappointment, and frustration threaten to invade your life.**

The people of Nineveh drifted back into the habit of doing things their way and ignoring God. As a result of ditching God's ways, they left themselves unprotected and open to attack from their enemies. Speaking through Nahum, God called them back to the protection of his will. God will be there for you when pain, disappointment, and frustration threaten to invade your life. When you feel like you are under attack, whether at home, at school, or at work, God offers you his protection. Nahum's message was this: God is good. Living within God's loving will puts you in the most secure position you can be.

If you choose to live outside God's boundaries, in a sense you're choosing also to live outside his protection. What areas of your life need to be brought within the walls of God's stronghold?

Seek the LORD while He may be found;
call upon Him while He is near.

ISAIAH 55:6 NKJV

Find God

You're young. You probably have a lot of life ahead of you. So when is a good time to get serious about seeking God? There's no better time than the present. "Seek the LORD while He may be found," said Isaiah. There's an urgency to that message. God is findable. Seek him. Don't let him get away—or, rather, don't let your life get away from you. The habits you establish now will be hard to break later. Get into the habit of seeking God now; if you don't—if you get settled into habits that don't include

God—he might not be so easy to find later.

Make it a habit to seek God in your daily activities. Seek God when you wake; seek God when you study or play or work. Seek God when you're with your friends and when you're among strangers.

At a conference, camp, or retreat God seems to be everywhere. At home afterward, when you dig into the busyness of everyday life, it may seem as if God is hard to find. This verse reminds you that God is near and that you can always find him.

It is important for you to know that God is near and will never leave you. God is near you at school and at home. God is near you even though no one else can see or no one else is looking. God is near when your friends are there for you and when your friends are gone. God is near you by the lockers and alongside the gossipers. God is everywhere, no matter where you are.

> God is near you even though no one else can see or no one else is looking.

How can you find God right here, right now? It is easy. God is near you this very minute. You will find God when you pray or talk to God.

God created human beings in his image. In the image of God he created them. He created them male and female.

GENESIS 1:27 NCV

You Have the Look

Clear skin. A perfect body. The right clothes. If you're like most teens, you spend a lot of time thinking about your appearance. It's no mystery why. Your peers have a habit of judging one another by appearances. On top of that, the media seem determined to convince you that your looks are the most important part of who you are. Think how many of the ads on TV are for things that are supposed to make you look better. TV shows are full of beautiful people. Magazine covers feature the hottest-looking guys or girls.

It may be hard to believe sometimes, but ultimately it doesn't much matter what other people think about the way you look. You are made in the image of God. You are patterned after the Creator of the universe, but not in the way you look. After all, you can't see God. It is your inner self that reflects God's image—your character, your creativity, your capacity for love.

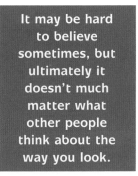

It may be hard to believe sometimes, but ultimately it doesn't much matter what other people think about the way you look.

Make it a habit to correct your "vision" when you check your image. Learn to see God in you. (He's there!) Learn to see what God loves about you.

When you look in a mirror, the image you see reflected there isn't the real you—certainly not the whole you. The most important reflection is not the one you see in the mirror; the most important is the reflection of God's image in your life. You have a lot to show the world: your heart and soul reflect the God of the universe. That's an image you can be proud of.

You are more than what you see in the mirror. If you really want to make an impression on people, show them what you've got inside.

God will wipe away every tear from their eyes, and there will be no more death, sadness, crying, or pain, because all the old ways are gone.

REVELATION 21:4 NCV

No More Tears

Chapter 21 in the book of Revelation is a visual and emotional masterpiece describing heaven. There are layers of precious stones including sapphire, emerald, topaz and more that form the foundation of the city. The city walls are pure gold. The streets are pure gold so polished that they appear to look like glass. There will be light everywhere. The light will come from God himself. The most incredible part of heaven may not be what you see; it may be what is missing that most demands your attention.

In heaven you will not find sin, Satan, or death. Anything in your present life that causes you pain, sadness, or even difficulty will vanish. Ignorance and misunderstanding will give way to complete understanding. Fear will be replaced by peace. Complete healing will occur, restoring every person. Nothing will wear out or decay; everything will be made whole and perfect. There will be no more good-byes. Best of all, death,

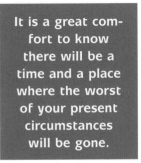

It is a great comfort to know there will be a time and a place where the worst of your present circumstances will be gone.

both natural and violent, will cease to exist. Tears will no longer be needed.

It is a great comfort to know there will be a time and a place where the worst of your present circumstances will be gone. For you, all the questions will be answered, and your faith will be complete. He will touch your face, wipe your tears, and welcome you to a joyful eternity.

Happy endings are not just a fairy tale. Ending up with God guarantees that you will live happily ever after and eternally with the One who loves you the most.

The LORD is with me like a strong warrior,
so those who are chasing me will trip and
fall; they will not defeat me.

JEREMIAH 20:11 NCV

He Will
Defend You

Do you ever feel picked on—like someone is out to hurt
you? Maybe a teacher has it in for you. Maybe a gossip is
spreading lies about you. Maybe a bully has chosen you for
a target.

Jeremiah knew a thing or two about that. The powers
that be in his society didn't appreciate his style of truth-
telling, and he found himself on their bad side. In fact, they

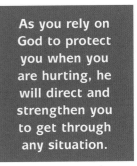

threw him in an empty cistern—a big, dark underground tank for storing rainwater—and left him there to die (until a friend came to rescue him). Another time he was thrown into the stocks for public humiliation. That's when Jeremiah spoke the words "The LORD is with me like a strong warrior, so those who are chasing me will trip and fall."

God was Jeremiah's defender, in spite of the trouble Jeremiah found himself in. God is your defender too, your strong warrior. It is good to know that God is your bodyguard, not so much in a physical sense, but more in the sense of helping you know how to handle tough situations. As you rely on God to protect you when you are hurting, he will direct and strengthen you to get through any situation. Your enemies will trip and fall while you stand firm. It may not be today, but you can trust in God's justice.

> **As you rely on God to protect you when you are hurting, he will direct and strengthen you to get through any situation.**

Lay your troubles before God, and see how he delivers you.

219

L<small>ORD</small>, I have heard the news about you; I am amazed at what you have done. L<small>ORD</small>, do great things once again in our time; make those things happen again in our own days. Even when you are angry, remember to be kind.

H<small>ABAKKUK</small> 3:2 NCV

God Will Amaze You

God has a pretty amazing reputation. Habakkuk had heard stories about how God had rescued his people from terrible trouble. Based on God's reputation, Habakkuk boldly asked God to do it again. In Habakkuk's prayer, recorded in chapter 3 verses 2–18, he recalled some of the incredible things God had done over time. By recounting the fantastic ways God had rescued his people in the past,

Habakkuk reassured himself that God would rescue his people again. Habakkuk recalled how in the past God caused an ocean to separate so God's people could walk safely across to the other side and avoid being captured by their enemies. Habakkuk prayed that God would do something of that magnitude to rescue the people of his time.

> God is an endless source of amazement. Be bold like Habakkuk and ask God to do for your generation what he has done in the past.

You can read about God's reputation throughout the Bible. It is a story that continues today because God continues to do amazing things. God listens to your prayers at any time of the day or night. He inspires people to write and record music for you to listen to. He causes the sun to rise and start each new day. God is an endless source of amazement. Be bold like Habakkuk and ask God to do for your generation what he has done in the past. Based on his reputation, you will not be disappointed with his response.

Write down a few of the fabulous ways you have been thrilled by God. Keep the list handy as a source of encouragement.

All those who stand before others and say they believe in me, I, the Son of Man, will say before the angels of God that they belong to me.

LUKE 12:8 NCV

Stand Up for Jesus

Jesus vigorously addressed hypocrisy—saying one thing and doing the opposite. Even the twelve disciples, who knew Jesus personally and walked with him every day for three years, fought with their own hypocrisy. It was difficult to say they believed that Jesus was the King, the Savior whom the Bible predicted. They risked imprisonment or death for what they believed. Jesus understood the danger they faced; he even knew they would deny knowing him at times. But he still expected them to love him and believe in him enough to fearlessly acknowledge and proclaim him as the Savior.

Jesus invested three years of his life teaching and training the disciples, knowing that after he was gone they would be the ones who continued to spread the word about God. He knew they would risk embarrassment, harassment, and even death to tell other people about his love and about his plan for every person. They needed to know how central they were to the survival of the truth about God.

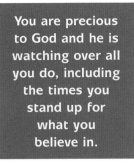

You are precious to God and he is watching over all you do, including the times you stand up for what you believe in.

You are precious to God and he is watching over all you do, including the times you stand up for what you believe in. God will watch over you when you step out of your comfort zone to tell others about God. As you talk about what you believe, you are continuing what the disciples bravely started.

Your voice raised in praise of who God is will be heard here on earth and in heaven. Shout out what you believe. Your words count.

Give freely to the poor person, and do not wish that you didn't have to give. The LORD your God will bless your work and everything you touch.

DEUTERONOMY 15:10 NCV

It Is Good to Give

If you've ever lifted weights, you understand the saying "No pain, no gain." You build muscle mass by pushing your muscles beyond what they can now do. Actually, you're making tiny tears in the muscle that are filled in with more muscle. And that hurts. Your ability to give grows in much the same way. When you give a little more than you thought you could—when you give till it hurts—God always fills in the gaps, bulks you up. And as you get stronger, it gets easier to do the heavy lifting that generosity requires.

You can give in different ways. You can give peace to your family by being ready on time to go on a family outing. You can give time to your church by helping out in the nursery. You can give comfort to your friends

> **When you give sacrificially, you put yourself in a position to watch God do amazing things.**

by listening to them. You can give support to someone in need by praying for that person. You can give pride to your community by picking up trash.

When you give more than you thought you could, you have to rely on the power of God to provide what you don't have. God always comes through, even if it's not in the same way you were expecting. When you give sacrificially, you put yourself in a position to watch God do amazing things. What better way to grow into a spiritual heavyweight yourself?

The more you give to God, the more blessings you receive. You can't outgive God, but it might be interesting and fun to try.

These things did not really come from me and my people. Everything comes from you; we have given you back what you gave us.

1 CHRONICLES 29:14 NCV

It All Belongs to God

"Mom, can I have five dollars?" The five-year-old boy looks expectantly into his mother's eyes. "What do you need with five dollars?" she asks. "I want to buy you a present." The mother, when she receives her son's five-dollar present, won't be five dollars ahead of the game. But that's not the point anyway. Her son's gift is an expression of his love for her. It's his way of saying he would love to shower her with gifts if only he could. That gesture does more to strengthen

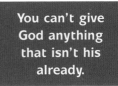

their relationship than any other exchange of goods and money could.

Any gift you offer up puts you in the position of that five-year-old boy. You can't give God anything that isn't his already. When you offer up your talents for God's service, you've giving back talents that came

> **You can't give God anything that isn't his already.**

from God. When you drop money in the offering plate, that's money God gave you first. And that's a wonderful expression of love for God.

The point isn't that you're helping God out. The point is that you're acknowledging that everything is his; by giving a portion of it back to him, you begin to appreciate even more the portion that he freely gives you to use. That expression of love is what pleases God and builds your relationship with him—not because you've met his needs, but because you have come to him like a child offering a gift of thanks to a loving Father.

It all belongs to God. God has given you all that you need to give to others; besides, you can't out give God.

To all who did accept him and believe in him he gave the right to become children of God.

JOHN 1:12 NCV

Become a Child of God

Christian music artist Geoff Moore will tell you that the moment he held Anna Grace in his arms, he had the clearest picture of what it meant to be a child of God. Geoff and his wife, Jan, traveled across miles and over oceans to claim their adopted daughter from an orphanage in China. To this day Geoff is moved with emotion when he describes how he was overwhelmed with love for this little girl whom he knew nothing about. It did not matter to him where she came from or where she was found. He is her father, and she is his child. That's the way it is with adoption. The child is deliberately chosen. Adoption is no accident or something that just happens. Adoption is an act of compassion and fulfillment and love.

God loves you more than you can imagine. Adoption is a picture of God's love for you. Your adoption is a new birth. You are not born again physically; you are born spiritually into God's family. You are his child, and he is your good Father.

Adoption is a picture of God's love for you. Your adoption is a new birth.

In addition to his everlasting, abundant love, he provides guidance and protection.

God accepts you as his child just the way you are. Just as Anna Grace did nothing to earn Geoff's and Jan's love, you don't need to do anything to earn God's love. Where you come from does not matter to him. What matters is that you reach out for him. He simply takes you into his arms and claims you as his child once and for all time.

Reach out to God with the heart of a child. He will welcome and love you as his very own.

Do not spread false rumors, and do not help a guilty person by giving false testimony.

EXODUS 23:1 GNT

Be Honest

If you've ever been the subject of a rumor at school, you know how a rumor can take on a life of its own. It races around the cafeteria and down the hallways like a lit fuse racing toward a stick of dynamite at the other end. Who knows what kind of damage it'll cause when the whole thing blows? Even the person who started the rumor—whether intentionally or unintentionally—has no control over it once it gets started.

When you spread a rumor, you are actually helping someone else hurt another person. You get yourself involved in someone else's guilt. Sure, it's hard to keep a juicy tidbit to yourself. But when you do resist the temptation to gossip—even more, when you refuse to believe bad things about another person without hard evidence—you make a big difference in the atmosphere around you. You are suddenly part of the solution rather than the problem.

God established laws that strengthen families, friends, and communities. At the heart of all good relationships is a trust built on honesty. Lies and rumors destroy trust and ignite all kinds of bad feelings like anger, revenge, and hate. Rumors and lies erode the foundation of honesty. God's laws are designed to ensure that people treat one another with fairness

When you spread a rumor, you are actually helping someone else hurt another person.

and honesty. Life is a lot easier when your parents and friends and teachers trust you. If you want to inspire that kind of trust, make honesty your goal at all times.

The next time you hear a hurtful rumor, take a stand: believe the best about others unless there's clear evidence that you shouldn't. You might be surprised at the impact you can have by refusing to pass along a rumor.

As pressure and stress bear down on me,
I find joy in your commands.

PSALM 119:143 NLT

From Stress to Joy

When the pressure and stress of life are building, joy is a welcome find. The pressure to fit in and the stress of grades and homework can get anyone down. Few people like to be told what to do, and yet when God asks you to do something, it's different. It's different because God asks you to do the things that will make your life easier and more enjoyable in the long run. His requests are based on his deep love and true concern for your life.

When Jesus was asked what the greatest commandment was, he replied that people should first love God and then love others. A practical example of how God's commands can bring you joy is found as you focus each day on loving God and loving others. Something happens when you turn the focus away from yourself. By

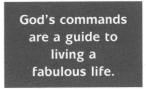

God's commands are a guide to living a fabulous life.

turning the focus on others, you spend less time stressing about yourself. Plus, it feels good to love other people.

God's instructions are a loving plan for a successful, enjoyable life. God knows the challenges you face. God asks you to love others as you would love yourself. He asks you to be honest and respectful. God wants you to put him first in your life. By following his directions, you will avoid and eliminate problems and confusion in your life. God's commands are a guide to living a fabulous life.

Living in your own strength is a good way to get worn down. Embrace God's plan for your life, and live in the joy it brings.

Jesus sat down and called the twelve apostles to him. He said, "Whoever wants to be the most important must be last of all and servant of all."

MARK 9:35 NCV

If You Want to Be First, Be Last

The disciples, the followers closest to Jesus, got caught arguing about which one of them was the greatest. Jesus had frequently shown them that following God wasn't about being great or first; it was about serving others and putting the needs of others first. To be great in God's kingdom, you have to put other people first and yourself last.

Putting others first is more than the occasional random act of kindness where you do something nice for someone. It is living your life with other people's needs first, not just sometime, but all the time. At home you might offer to fix a meal for your family, or you could consider your family's schedule first before making your own plans. At school you could invite someone who normally sits alone to sit with you and your friends. Putting others first involves listening and hearing what they really need. Putting others first requires treating everyone equally regardless of their status, their past, or popular opinion. In addition to putting others first, you can go a step further by serving others too.

Putting others first requires treating everyone equally regardless of their status, their past, or popular opinion.

By putting others first, you will be in a position to serve others. Make it your goal to serve instead of being served. God's love comes alive for other people when you serve them. You become a living example of God's love. As you selflessly serve others, you will become the kind of great person that Jesus was hoping for in his disciples. You will be a great servant of others.

If you put others first, logically speaking you will be last. Get at the end of the line and see what needs to be done for the people in front of you.

GOD told Samuel, "Looks aren't everything. Don't be impressed with his looks and stature. I've already eliminated him. GOD judges persons differently than humans do. Men and women look at the face; GOD looks into the heart."

1 SAMUEL 16:7 MSG

Not Just Looks

Jock. Geek. Queen bee. Stoner. Snob. If you can figure out what category to stick a person in, that's all you need to know. Or is it? Categories don't tell you anything about what's inside a person. And yet that's who a person really is. Heart, character, soul—they're all on the inside. The inside is what God sees when he looks at a person.

When the prophet Samuel went to Jesse's house looking for the next king of Israel, he put young David in the same categories that David's family put him in: the little brother, the shepherd boy, certainly no king. But God told Samuel to look again. In David's heart, God saw the man who would lead his people to greatness.

> When you put people in a category, you've written them off, as if you've got them all figured out.

Sure, it's hard—maybe impossible—to see what's inside another person. But that's the point. When you put people in a category, you've written them off, as if you've got them all figured out: she fits in Category X, so I know she's going to do this, believe that, and feel that other thing. But people are never that simple. On the inside, they're just as complicated as you are.

So be careful when you dismiss another person with a flippant "I know his type." Samuel and Jesse and David's brothers thought they knew David's type, but he was one in a million. So are you. So is everybody you've ever known.

—

Pick one of the social groups at your school—one of the groups that you think you "know their type." Commit to get to know at least one of those people as an individual.

Be kind and loving to each other, and forgive each other just as God forgave you in Christ.

EPHESIANS 4:32 NCV

Forgive Because He Forgave You

Paul challenged believers to treat one another as God treated them. Whether people deserve it or not, they should be treated with kindness. If God can love and forgive you, then you, too, can love and forgive others.

Jesus lived out this principle. Zacchaeus overcharged people on their taxes and kept the profits for himself. No one liked that dishonest, greedy man, but Jesus went to his home and shared a meal with him. As a result of that small kindness, Zacchaeus changed his ways and dedicated himself to living more like Jesus. On another occasion, Jesus shared a conversation with a woman at a well. He asked her for a drink of water. This woman had a bad reputation. Their conversation inspired her to change her life and share all Jesus told her with the people in her village. As a result, not only was her life changed, but the people of her village believed in Jesus too. Jesus accepted the most unacceptable people. No matter what a person did or was, Jesus offered forgiveness and the opportunity to live a new life.

There is nothing that gets a person's attention more quickly than showing undeserved kindness to him.

There is nothing that gets a person's attention more quickly than showing undeserved kindness to him. At school or work there might be someone who has hurt you or who is regarded as unacceptable. The kindness and forgiveness Jesus offered to you changed your life. By extending forgiveness to others, you can help change lives too.

If you find it hard to forgive other people, remember what God has forgiven you.

Always remember what is written in the Book of the Teachings. Study it day and night to be sure to obey everything that is written there. If you do this, you will be wise and successful in everything.

JOSHUA 1:8 NCV

More Than Words

Following the rules can be hard for a teen. You feel you're ready to be independent and do things your own way, but your parents and teachers and bosses are still trying to control you with rules that can seem arbitrary or unfair.

Sure, some rules really are arbitrary or unfair. But most rules exist for a good reason. Take the rules of the road.

They are limiting. They don't let you drive on the left side of the road or on the sidewalk. But if you keep within the few limits of the law, you have the freedom to drive wherever you want to. The laws are there to protect everyone's freedom, not to take it away.

The same is true of God's laws. They don't exist to spoil your fun, but to ensure that you succeed. That's why God told Joshua to study his teaching day and night and to obey it—so he would be wise and success-ful. God wants the same thing for you. Within God's guidelines there is tremendous freedom to live a happy and fulfilling life. Step outside those guidelines, and you might run into a head-on collision.

> **Within God's guidelines there is tremendous freedom to live a happy and fulfilling life.**

It's human nature to question the rules. Every now and then, it might even be appropriate to speak up and challenge human rules that seem unfair or not well thought out. But you can be sure that God's rules exist to lead you on to greater happiness. God's laws are just part of his love for you.

God's laws are more than simply rules to memorize; God's laws are the way he cares for you. Allow God to show you how much he loves you by reading his laws in the Bible.

If someone obeys God's teaching, then in that person God's love has truly reached its goal.

1 JOHN 2:5 NCV

You Know
You Belong

When you fall in love, no one has to tell you to talk to that person every day. You do it to be near that person and to be a part of that person's life. The person you are in love with doesn't have to tell you what to do to please him or her. You make it your mission to know what pleases the person you love, and you do it. Doing things the way your boyfriend or girlfriend wants is not a chore, it's a joy. In a similar way, your response to God's love leads to obedience. It isn't forced. Obedience is your voluntary surrender to the goodness of God's ways.

The irony of obedience is that the more you know about God, the more you are motivated to make sure that nothing separates you from him. His ways represent the best life has to offer you.

Be sure that you have turned control of your life over to God. John said that your willingness to comply with the laws and the guidance God provides for your life is evidence of your love for God. If your obedience is a result of your own ability to follow rules, you have missed out on what God intended. As you fall in love with God, his laws and direction will cease

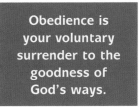

Obedience is your voluntary surrender to the goodness of God's ways.

to be rules and will become a gift of love. Your complete surrender to him is your assurance that his love is being made perfect in you.

Answer honestly: Do you work harder at pleasing yourself or pleasing God? Your obedience is evidence of what really matters to you.

The tongue is a small part of the body, but it brags about great things. A big forest fire can be started with only a little flame.

JAMES 3:5 NCV

The Power of Words

One sentence, even one word, has the power to heal or hurt. Imagine walking through the school parking lot and overhearing your name. Though you keep walking, your ears tune in, hoping to hear a kind word, but there is also a concern that you are about to be slammed. Sometimes school seems like a soap opera that plays out with exaggerated words, lies, and half-truths.

James gave an account of how powerful words could be. He used three analogies to make his point. Most horses weigh from eight hundred to one thousand–plus pounds and are strong enough to plow fields or carry a full-grown man for miles. Yet, the horse is controlled with one small piece of metal called a bit and a leather bridle that fits over the horse's head. You can harness the wild strength of a horse with something that a horse could trample. Like the bit and bridle, the rudder on a ship is small in comparison to the ship itself, but it is the rudder that steers the ship one direction or another. Even smaller than the rudder is a tiny spark. Although it is tiny, a spark alone has the ability to start a blaze.

> Words reflect the true condition of a person's heart and maturity.

Your tongue, the words you say, steer your life in one direction or another. Like the spark, one offhand remark can do major damage. Words reflect the true condition of a person's heart and maturity. Make sure your verbal contributions are uplifting, encouraging, and honest.

Be the one to spread good news about others. Use your words to build people up. Your carefully chosen words can even heal someone who is hurting.

Faith means being sure of the things we hope for and knowing that something is real even if we do not see it.

HEBREWS 11:1 NCV

Attempting to Define Faith

Faith isn't an easy word to define because faith is an indefinable quality that goes beyond words. The New Testament was originally written in the Greek language. In that original text it said that *faith* is "the substance of things hoped and the evidence of things not seen." The word *substance* in Greek is *hupostatis*, which means a structure under something, a foundation, a steadfastness of mind. Faith is the firm foundation on which you rest everything you know about God.

The Bible provides knowledge and history about God. It is filled with truth that is not changed by circumstances. The Bible clearly states who God is, that he is truth and holiness. He doesn't change. Knowing who God is and knowing about his character is not enough. The Bible says even demons know who God is.

Without faith you would be limited to the here and now. You would know God only by what you could see, hear, touch, taste, and smell. There is so much about God that goes beyond your limited human senses. No one was present for creation. It was something God did alone. The Holy Spirit is unseen and can't be touched or heard or smelled or tasted. You can't use your own abilities to define and know faith. Faith is grounded in the truth of the Bible. Faith is accepting your experience with God while combining it with the certainty of the Bible.

Faith is accepting your experience with God while combining it with the certainty of the Bible.

Are you putting your faith in what you can see with your eyes, or in what you know to be true from the Bible? Faith isn't just wishful thinking. It's substantial. It's strong enough to build a life on.

Do not be fooled: "Bad friends will ruin good habits."

1 Corinthians 15:33 ncv

Friends Reflect Who You Are

Friendships are usually based on acceptance. You will gravitate toward the people who accept you. Acceptance could cause your friends to choose you rather than you choosing your friends. Make a conscious effort to choose your friends rather than just choosing acceptance.

Real friends don't just accept you, they love you. Friends have each other's best interests at heart. Friends care enough to be honest and to build each other up. A true friend will risk losing you as a friend in order to confront issues in your life that are harmful or destructive to you. A true friend will value you more than the friendship.

Your friends have more influence on you than anyone else in your life. Just ask Cole. He hangs his head and admits that he can make the right choices, until he gets around a certain group of friends. They make it too easy and daring to do the wrong thing. Friends who share your standards and your

Your friends have more influence on you than anyone else in your life.

beliefs will encourage you in a positive way. Friends who don't share your standards and beliefs are more likely to cause you to fall away from your beliefs than to rise up to yours. You can influence friends who don't know about God by including them in your circle of godly friends rather than spending all your time with their friends. Choose your friends wisely.

Friends are a reflection of who you are and what you stand for. Good friends can bring out the best in you. Take time to evaluate whom you are friends with and why.

We know that a person is made right with God not by following the law, but by trusting in Jesus Christ. So we, too, have put our faith in Christ Jesus, that we might be made right with God because we trusted in Christ. It is not because we followed the law, because no one can be made right with God by following the law.

GALATIANS 2:16 NCV

Follow Jesus

Think about the rules that govern behavior in your school. They help teachers and administrators maintain order by giving them a standard to hold students' conduct against. Most students are there to learn and to get along with their peers, but for those who don't share that attitude, the rules serve as an external motivation to behave as if they did. If all students treated their teachers and fellow students with love, always treated others the way they would want to be treated themselves, there would be no need for rules.

Of course, since nobody's perfect, rules are necessary. But even if the rules can cause people to behave well, no set of rules can make much change on the inside of a person. Not even God's laws do that. God's laws are a standard for how you should behave toward other people. If you follow the laws of

If you obey God's law perfectly, you will behave like a perfectly loving human being.

God, you will be doing your part toward creating a just and orderly world. If you obey God's laws perfectly, you will behave like a perfectly loving human being.

But the laws of God serve another purpose. They show you how far you have to go. Every time you break one of God's laws—and you will—you are faced with the fact that you can't do it on your own. You see that you need a new heart. Only God can reach into your life and make you into the kind of person the laws say you ought to be.

Trust Jesus to give you a new heart—a heart that truly desires to follow God's laws.

I don't care about my own life. The most important thing is that I complete my mission, the work that the Lord Jesus gave me—to tell people the Good News about God's grace.

ACTS 20:24 NCV

Worth Telling About

Paul prepared to go to a place where he knew he would be imprisoned and beaten, maybe even killed, for his beliefs. None of these things deterred him from going. Paul would rather face pain and imprisonment than give up his task of telling people about Jesus. To Paul life was worthless if he couldn't be telling others about Jesus.

Paul knew that without Jesus in their lives, people would be separated from God forever. And being separated from God prevented them from living life to the fullest. It was the most important thing people needed to know.

In some countries today there are places where it is illegal to talk about your faith in Jesus. The Christian Church functions in underground home churches. There are even places where pastors and Christians are imprisoned for talking about their faith. At the same time, the number of new Christians is growing at an astounding rate in these places. The

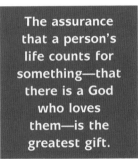

The assurance that a person's life counts for something—that there is a God who loves them—is the greatest gift.

people in those countries know that it is worth risking their lives to spread the love of God. They know that God introduces forgiveness and mercy into life as they embrace the unconditional love he offers. In good times and in bad, the assurance that a person's life counts for something—that there is a God who loves them—is the greatest gift.

Someone is dying to know about the love of God. Share what you know about God.

et us run the race that is before us and never give up. We should remove from our lives anything that would get in the way and the sin that so easily holds us back.

HEBREWS 12:1 NCV

Don't Stop

In addition to the athletes on a track team, there is a coach. The coach evaluates the condition of each athlete's form and physical condition. He is responsible for helping the athlete improve his race performance, which includes disciplining and correcting the athlete. The author of Hebrews suggests that you look at your relationship with God from the perspective of a runner in a race with God as your coach.

Like the runner in a race, set your sights on the finish line, which in your case is the end of your life on earth. Set a training schedule that includes spiritual discipline. Prayer and worship are two spiritual disciplines you may be familiar with. Fasting is also a spiritual discipline you may have heard of; fasting is the decision to give up something that is important to you for a set period of time in order to focus on God. For

> **Stick to a good training schedule, and, above all, listen to your coach—God.**

instance, you could give up your favorite TV program for a month and use the time to do a Bible study.

If your goal is to stay on track with your relationship to God, then be like the runner and do not let anything distract you from getting to the finish line. Take the time to figure out what might get you off track in your relationship with God. Get rid of the things that tear down your relationship with him, and allow only those things that build it up. Stick to a good training schedule, and, above all, listen to your coach—God.

If you aren't in training, you can't hope to be much of a racer. Get serious about seeking God: keep your eyes on Jesus, and the finish line.

They traded the truth of God for a lie. They worshiped and served what had been created instead of the God who created those things, who should be praised forever.

ROMANS 1:25 NCV

Worship God

Worship is your reverence, your honor toward something. Worship is committing your life to whatever you love the most. Worship is more than a church service or music. Worship is a lifestyle that reflects with honor the One you love the most.

Paul, the writer of Romans, retold the tragedy of what happened in the Old Testament when Christians became frustrated or impatient with God. If God didn't do what they thought he should, they found other things to worship. As a result, they drifted away from God. They became consumed by their own selfish desires. Paul warned the Christians in Rome to worship God and not the things God created for them.

You can choose to make the most ordinary tasks in your day an act of worship by doing them with excellence.

The Bible tells about all kinds of ways people worshiped God. Worship in Bible times included Scripture reading, music, teaching, dancing, extended periods of silence, and prayer. Praise music and friends all around can enhance a worship experience, but worship is more than the experience. Worship is your response to God's power and grace and love. If you truly love God, your worship of him will overflow into your daily life. Your words and your actions will become a form of worship to God. You can choose to make the most ordinary tasks in your day an act of worship by doing them with excellence.

Worship God when you brush your teeth in the morning; teeth are a gift from God. Worship God when you lay your head on your pillow tonight; thank him for another day.

Run away from sexual sin. Every other sin people do is outside their bodies, but those who sin sexually sin against their own bodies. You should know that your body is a temple for the Holy Spirit who is in you. You have received the Holy Spirit from God. So you do not belong to yourselves.

1 CORINTHIANS 6:18–19 NCV

Worth the Wait

You're tired of waiting for a cake to come out of the oven, so you decide to snatch it out and dip into the half-baked batter with a spoon. If someone prevented you from carrying out your plan, you might consider that person a party pooper, intent on spoiling your fun. But isn't it just as likely that this person, instead of trying to spoil your enjoyment of the cake, is actually trying to enhance it? You might think you want cake batter, but that's just because you aren't in touch with how good cake can be when it's done right. If you wait for the cake to be ready, you'll be very glad you did.

You live in a highly sexualized culture. From the things you see on television and movies to the articles in magazines to the clothes your peers wear, sex—however you can get it—is portrayed as the key to personal fulfillment and self-expression. So when you learn that the Bible

The Bible doesn't teach that sex is bad. It teaches that it's good— too good to be thrown away.

forbids sex outside marriage, you might perceive God as a cosmic party pooper determined to spoil the fun of sex.

But isn't it possible that God is just the opposite? Maybe God's laws are designed to heighten your enjoyment of sex by ensuring that you don't settle for a cheapened, half-baked version. The Bible doesn't teach that sex is bad. It teaches that it's good—too good to be thrown away. Sex is good enough to be worth the wait.

One of the greatest gifts God gives is sexual intimacy within a marriage. It is your job to protect that gift for your future marriage partner.

Jesus said to me, "My grace is enough for you. When you are weak, my power is made perfect in you." So I am very happy to brag about my weaknesses. Then Christ's power can live in me.

2 CORINTHIANS 12:9 NCV

He Can Use Your Weakness

Paul discovered the secret to dealing with the unpleasant things in life. He decided to treat his weakness and difficulties as a gift from God. He could do this because he realized the weaker he became, the more he had to depend on God's strength. Paul asked God to take away his weakness, but God chose to leave it. Paul's weakness strengthened his relationship with God. God did not take Paul's difficulties away; God helped Paul deal with them.

Difficulties and challenges are a good thing; they are opportunities to allow God to do things he wouldn't otherwise do. You may face difficulties in your life that you wish God would just take away. God may supply what you need to make it through your difficulties rather than remove them. For example, a father will take his child to the doctor and allow that child to be given what appears to the child as a big,

> God may supply what you need to make it through your difficulties rather than remove them.

painful shot. A child will not understand why his father allowed someone to hurt him until he is older and realizes that shots can make you well or keep you from getting sick. Remember that God sees beyond your moment of suffering.

When you ask for God's help, you gain the chance to see all the things he can do. Take your difficulties and weaknesses to God in prayer. Ask him to use them in a way that reveals his strength and greatness.

You may think of your point of weakness as the last place where God can work through your life. Have you ever considered the possibility that it might be the precise spot where God plans to work? Commit even your weaknesses and failures to God's good work.

All people will know that you are my followers if you love each other.

JOHN 13:35 NCV

Be Known by Your Love

In the Old Testament, the people of God followed laws designed to help them be holy and to set them apart from other religions. There were laws for every aspect of life to ensure that people were doing their best to live a holy and separate life. These requirements failed to keep God's people separate. They lost their meaning and became routine. Jesus gave a new law or command that summed up the Old Testament law: love others. Your friends and family will know you are a follower of God by how you love people.

Scientific research suggests that every human being requires love, but you don't need scientists to tell you that. The evidence is up and down the hallways of your school. People display their need for love in a variety of ways, from clothes that stand out to the R-rated displays

> Loving others will set you apart far more than any Christian symbol, jewelry, or T-shirt you can wear.

of public affection. Anyone with an authentic love for other people will get noticed.

Loving others will set you apart far more than any Christian symbol, jewelry, or T-shirt you can wear. Love isn't something you talk about; it's something you do when you treat everyone equally. Real love happens when you take time to listen to someone who is hurting. Being a good listener and offering to pray with someone about a problem shows love too. Love others in the same unrestricted way God loves you, and leave no doubt about your relationship with God.

When you love people without any conditions or exceptions, people will notice. Let love for others be your ID.

I heard the voice of the Lord, saying: "Whom shall I send, and who will go for Us?" Then I said, "Here am I! Send me."

ISAIAH 6:8 NKJV

Send Me

When you have some good news — a big sale at the mall, a new band you've discovered, a big win for your favorite team — you don't hesitate to tell people. Are you just as eager to tell people the news that God loves them and has a plan for their lives? When God asked the prophet Isaiah to go and tell people about the God who loved them, Isaiah realized his job wouldn't be easy. It would require sacrifice and make him unpopular at times. Nevertheless, Isaiah said yes to God.

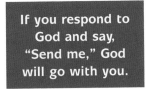

God asks you to go and tell other people about him. You may not have to go far, possibly just into your own living room to tell someone in your family about God. You may get the opportunity to tell a friend at school about God. Telling others about God doesn't involve only words. Sure, talking about God is a great way to let others know about him. But you can also let others know about God by your actions. You can share God's message by lending a hand in your own city. You might go to a food bank and help unload donated food for the poor people in your city. You may even be challenged to go on a mission trip to another country.

> **If you respond to God and say, "Send me," God will go with you.**

If you respond to God and say, "Send me," God will go with you. God will be there when you talk to your family and friends and when you work in your community. God will be along for the ride if you decide to go on a mission trip. Your willingness to put God's plans for your life before your own is the response God will be looking for.

Start planning a way to put your belief in God into action. Include in your action plan a list of people in your life right now who might not know about God's love.

Give all your worries to him, because he cares about you.

1 PETER 5:7 NCV

No Worries;
God Cares

There will be times in life when you feel that no one cares and no one is listening. It can hit you in a crowd at school or standing next to your family at church. It isn't out of the question to feel lonely even when you are not alone. In those moments it is crucial to set your thoughts on what the Bible says rather than be drawn in by the emotion of loneliness.

Often it is worry that drives you to isolate yourself. Pulling away from God and from the people who could support you is a natural reaction to pain and difficulty. Paul addressed this type of situation in his letter to a group of very discouraged Christians. Those people were being threatened, beaten, imprisoned, and even killed for believing Jesus was the Son of God and the eternal King. They felt abandoned by God. Paul urged them not to submit to circumstance and emotion, but to remain confident in the truth they had heard and witnessed.

You can safely hand over your worry to God and be absolutely confident he cares.

Paul went on to say that it is the enemy, Satan, who wants to destroy faith with worry and isolation. The truth is, God loves you. Any worry you have is a concern to him. You can safely hand over your worry to God and be absolutely confident he cares. Despite what the enemy would like you to believe, you are not alone. The worries that threaten to overwhelm you will never overwhelm God.

Lighten your load of worries by sharing them with the ones who love you. Start with the One who loves you most — God. Give him what is getting you down.

IMPORTANT
BIBLE VERSES
FOR LEADERS

$\mathbf{D}$o to others what you would
want them to do to you.

You who are younger must follow your leaders. But all of you, leaders and followers alike, are to be down to earth with each other, for—God has had it with the proud, but takes delight in just plain people.

1 PETER 5:5 MSG

Be the Leader You Want to Follow

Some of the most loved presidents have been those described as "just plain people." They were approachable, genuine, real, and down-to-earth. Followers want a leader with whom they can relate, and who can relate to them. You may not be president of a nation or even a corporation, but because you have influence, it is important for you to be sincerely concerned for others while being yourself. The higher up you go in leadership, the easier it becomes to isolate

yourself from the others whom you are leading. You may find it equally as challenging to associate with executives in the morning as with your children in the evening. By remaining authentic, you can face the challenges successfully.

Jesus Christ was the greatest of all leaders. He could have easily used his positional power and separated himself from others. Instead, he embraced people and even served his disciples by washing their feet in an act of humility as told in the Gospel of John. He was an authentic servant leader.

> **By remaining authentic, you can face the challenges successfully.**

The irony in working with many different types of people is that as long as you are trying to fit in with the crowd, you will be disconnected from them. God has created you with a unique personality. When you honor him and yourself by being authentic, a natural connection with other people opens to you.

Examine your authenticity. When you act out of the natural personality and gifts God created in you, you will begin to feel at ease in your relationships . . . and so will others.

Wisdom that is from above is first pure, then peaceable, gentle, willing to yield, full of mercy and good fruits, without partiality and without hypocrisy.

JAMES 3:17 NKJV

Leadership Lifestyle

The higher you are in a position of leadership, the broader your influence will become on others and the more pervasive the responsibility will be on your life. When you accept the role of a leader, you accept the responsibility of influencing others. Maybe you did not realize you were signing up for a lifestyle when you agreed to lead the church committee or accepted the promotion at work. But leadership is not a job; it is a lifestyle.

Lifestyle leadership requires godly wisdom. Therefore, the wisdom described in James 3:17 is important for you

because it presents a hierarchy or ladder of wise traits for the leader. Each characteristic builds upon the previous one and must be an integrated and true part of your lifestyle.

You cultivate a pure motive and character, which enables you to bring peace to others. You can then add peace with fairness to everyone in a situation. As you evolve as a wise leader, you will care for those in need and help meet their needs through your good deeds for them. As this display of wisdom becomes ingrained in

> **Leadership is not a job; it is a lifestyle.**

your lifestyle, you will become more unwavering and genuine in your leadership in every area of your life. Leadership is not a role that you play, but an expression of your wisdom to benefit others. The higher you climb in leadership, the less room you have for anonymity and conformity and the more room you have to influence others to greatness.

Make a list of ten people, including family, friends, and colleagues, whom you most influence regularly. Pray and ask God to show you how to be an even wiser influence on each person.

$\mathbb{T}$he eyes of the LORD are in every place, keeping watch on the evil and the good.

PROVERBS 15:3 NKJV

Hidden Cameras

Many days offer moments when you are sure that *Candid Camera* must be taping you. Some days things just go awry, or you may even be the one to go off-kilter. Leaders have their share of opportunities to make innocent mistakes, moral blunders, and ethical compromises. You may have privately experienced moments of decision or emotion that you would not want to share publicly.

Fortunately, every minute of the leader's day is not caught on tape to be scrutinized by others. However, there is a constant audience keeping watch on evil and good alike. So, how do you keep yourself accountable without placing every decision on display for others to judge? Remember that your most important audience is God. He watches your misdeeds and mistakes for sure, but he sees them through a lens of mercy. The great news is that he doesn't limit his viewing to the embarrassing scenes that you would rather forget.

> God sees you when you give a simple compliment to the sometimes-overlooked receptionist.

God is not a faultfinder. He is not watching, waiting only for a leader's indiscretion; he also watches for good. He sees you when you take a stand for righteousness. God sees you when you give a simple compliment to the sometimes-overlooked receptionist. He sees all the deeds that others in your organization may not be able to see. God sees all, and he is admiring your good works too.

⁓

You should review your bloopers and blunders each day. Look at the hidden camera recordings, viewing as God does with mercy. Correct your mistakes daily, and commend your successes also.

Those who built on the wall, and those who carried burdens, loaded themselves so that with one hand they worked at construction, and with the other held a weapon. Every one of the builders had his sword girded at his side as he built.

NEHEMIAH 4:17–18 NKJV

Two-Fisted Leadership

An effective leader spurs progress. But you must understand that progress brings change and change sometimes brings adversity. You can handle the distraction of adversity by following Nehemiah's example. Nehemiah was a leader with a mission to rebuild the wall of ancient Jerusalem, which would provide protection, privacy, and prosperity for his followers. But as with all leaders, Nehemiah faced adversaries. His adversity came from both the outside competition and his own people inside.

Nehemiah's is an ideal and important example for you because he faced mockery, ridicule, doubt, even physical threats against his mission. By example, Nehemiah tells the leader how to handle adversity—work two-fisted. With a brick in one hand, Nehemiah continued to build the wall and equipped his team to build with him. He continued with forward progress while he addressed the challengers. In the other hand, he held a weapon. Now, as a leader you might not literally hold a weapon today, but you can be prepared and equipped for the battle. Nehemiah did not ignore the insults or naively underestimate the adversary. He did realize the seriousness of the battle and stayed in a protective and defensive stance.

> **Equip and empower your team to build success in the face of adversity.**

As a leader, you can follow this example. When you know that a change is inevitable or needed, use two-fisted leadership. Equip and empower your team to build success in the face of adversity. Establish your purpose, present your plan, and protect your process to accomplish your vision.

Examine today's biggest challenge. Write down what tools you will use to continue progress and what methods you will utilize to address challenges. Then keep moving in forward progress.

Get advice if you want your plans to
work. If you go to war, get the advice of
others.

PROVERBS 20:18 NCV

Safety in
Numbers

Even the Lone Ranger had Tonto. Whether you are the
top leader in your own organization or a homemaker leading your children, you endure difficult decisions with challenging choices. Often, even when you have prayed, listed
your pros and cons, and given much thought to the matter,
you are still lacking clear direction for your decision. You
must remember that God hears every prayer. Sometimes he
answers you directly, and sometimes he counsels through
others' advice.

A leader is wise to develop a system of getting advice.
You may form an advisory board, leadership team, account-

ability group, or circle of friends. Whatever you want to name it, you need a small group of trusted advisers who can share their wisdom with you in your decision-making process.

An effective GROUP of advisers offers: **G**odly wisdom, **R**ealism, **O**ptimism, **U**nderstanding, and **P**erseverance. Be sure to invite godly wisdom. God's truths are universal and have been proved successful. Advice should line up with the Word of God and be prayerfully given. A realist will give you a perspective of the good, the bad, and the ugly; whereas an optimist will give you the bright side of possi-

> You need a small group of trusted advisors who can share their wisdom with you in your decision-making process.

bilities. It is wise to keep a balance of both. With a strong understanding of your mission and vision, an adviser will help to keep you on the path you want to travel. Finally, your group should be persevering. A strong group of advisers provides the safety in numbers you need as a leader.

Examine how the five most influential people in your life fit into your GROUP. If some GROUP roles are missing, pray and ask God to direct you in relationships that will fill those voids.

Think of ways to encourage one another to outbursts of love and good deeds.

HEBREWS 10:24 NLT

Setting the Tone

Even though most people appreciate materialistic rewards, they are not satisfied with material perks or financial gain alone. Since Elton Mayo's Hawthorne Studies around 1930, leaders have understood that workers are more influenced by social demands, the need for recognition, and a sense of belonging than they are by raises and bonuses. You set the tone for the atmosphere that will meet the real needs of the people under your influence. You can learn how to create an atmosphere that will motivate people to achieve company or family goals while attaining personal fulfillment by encouraging acts of love and kindness among others.

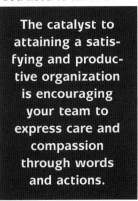

The catalyst to attaining a satisfying and productive organization is encouraging your team to express care and compassion through words and actions. You need to think of ways to encourage this setting. It will not develop on its own, but must be intentional. Your list of strategies to set the tone might include a meditation or Scripture of the day, the celebration of birthdays and achievements, a company coffee club for breaks, special team lunches, family wellness plans, and flexible compensation time. The company newsletter, e-mail groups, team meetings, and family dinners are good avenues to disperse encouragement with little or no cost to the organization.

> **The catalyst to attaining a satisfying and productive organization is encouraging your team to express care and compassion through words and actions.**

Your initiative and intention in setting the tone will reap many rewards for your organization. When you strive to meet the personal needs of your followers, your organization will develop stronger unity and a more loyal and satisfied team.

Make a decision to unify your team. Then, establish a new tradition that provides an opportunity for your team to engage in conversation and compassion.

With that kind of hope to excite us, nothing holds us back.

2 Corinthians 3:12 msg

Surplus Dreams

Do you live in the comfort zone of your capability, or do you dare to dream in your role as a leader? A leader's ability to have the biggest dreams of anyone in your organization is significant. When you plan, make it a three-pronged plan by setting a goal, marking a hope, and daring a dream.

Carry your goals all the way through to attaining your dreams. Goal setting is familiar to leaders. Goals should be attainable but challenging for your organization. Once you

have set your goal, next mark your hope. What do you really hope you will achieve if everyone is working to his or her best capability? The final prong of planning is more daring. What do you dream? What is the impossible that you would be foolish to say aloud? When you know this is impossible in your own power and capability—you

> **Surplus planning almost guarantees success above and beyond your original goal.**

have arrived at exceeding, abundant thinking. God can do even more than that for you and through you.

In your three-pronged planning, motivate your entire organization by sharing your goals, hopes, and dreams. Surplus planning almost guarantees success above and beyond your original goal. It raises the standard of excellence without burdening your followers (or yourself) with undue pressure. God is able to step into your organization and do the dream—even above what you can imagine or request.

⌇

Examine your organizational goals. Can you press them a little further? Take a daring approach and plan beyond your stated goal. Show exceeding, abundant thinking in your plan.

The LORD says, "Forget what happened before, and do not think about the past. Look at the new thing I am going to do. It is already happening. Don't you see it? I will make a road in the desert and rivers in the dry land."

ISAIAH 43:18–19 NCV

Caution: Bridge Under Construction

Change happens. In fact, change is one consistent characteristic of all progress. Think of the transportation system. At times roads need reconstruction because the asphalt has deteriorated and potholes have formed. Other roads need reconstruction because of economic growth that increases traffic and requires expansion of the roadways. A detour, bridge, or some other change agent will be required in the transition through the change—and even though there is hope for safer and faster travel, the drivers usually get frustrated in the process.

Whether propelled by failure or success, change is inevitable. You must be a change agent if you are going to be an effective and progressive leader. Change begins with a vision of something better. So often leaders have great vision for their organization and share the vision of progress with their followers, expecting everyone to jump on board, ready

> **You have the exciting privilege of stirring enthusiasm for the new vision.**

to enjoy the ride. As change agent, you should expect resistance among those who will be part of the change. But you have the exciting privilege of stirring enthusiasm for the new vision.

Focusing on the "new thing," you lay out the plan for addressing change. You are the change agent—the temporary road or detour that moves people from the old system to the new one. You can relieve the sense of anxiety, create a sense of possibility, and instill an attitude of adventure among the people involved in the change by sharing a vision of something greater to come.

— ◈ —

If you have a process that is not working well in your organization, envision a better way. Write down the vision. Make a plan to communicate the vision and construct the change.

Your beauty should come from within you—the beauty of a gentle and quiet spirit that will never be destroyed and is very precious to God.

1 PETER 3:4 NCV

Invisible Vogue

As you prepare to enter the most important presentation of the week, you check the mirror. You find that your newest Hugo Boss tie or St. John suit looks as sharp as it did in the magazine. With meticulous hair, manicured nails, and perfectly whitened teeth, you acknowledge that you will make a perfect first impression.

You need to make a positive impression on others, so it is easy to get caught up in the newest look or hottest label of cutting-edge fashion. Unfortunately, that perfect look isn't permanent. The clothes will wear, the hair will gray, the nails will break, and the teeth will stain again. Maintaining the look of a leader is more about cultivating character than charisma.

> **Maintaining the look of a leader is more about cultivating character than charisma.**

It is important for you to cultivate true beauty that never fades. One might expect a leader to be described as a "mover and shaker," rather than "gentle and quiet in spirit." Insight reveals "gentle" as a type of reliance on God to defend your injustices, and "quiet" as being steadfast in spirit. When you become confident enough to know that you do not have to defend every decision, and you are secure with your own God-given abilities, you exude the beauty of character that radiates from within and is precious to God. Take as much time cultivating inner beauty as you do creating outer beauty, and you will make a positive and lasting first impression not only on many, but on God as well.

〜

Conduct a character checkup today. If there is an area in which you are not relying on God to resolve a situation, pray and commit it to him.

Words kill, words give life; they're either poison or fruit—you choose.

PROVERBS 18:21 MSG

Sticks and Stones

"Sticks and stones may break my bones, but words will never hurt me." If you remember this nursery rhyme, you probably also remember the words to which you were responding. In fact, even children know that words do hurt. Often you realize the importance of words when you are the victim of a hurtful comment, even as an adult. Seldom do you realize how hurtful words are when you are the one speaking them.

You must realize that your words are powerful and carry great influence. Words can give life or kill it. You have a choice. With your words, you can stifle effectiveness in your organization. Or you can inspire momentum, impart courage, and instill hope. If a once-loyal partner leaves your organization, choose to impart hope for new opportunities. If someone makes a risky decision that fails, choose to comfort him and encourage his continued innovation.

> **With your words you can stifle effectiveness in your organization. Or you can inspire momentum, impart courage, and instill hope.**

Words have consequences, and you must accept those consequences. Begin your conversation with the end result in mind. You must choose what you want to cultivate in your relationship. You will reap what you sow, even through your speaking. So, speak life and reap life. Give encouragement; receive encouragement. Be a friend; find a friend. In choosing your response, you choose your consequence.

~※

Give yourself three to five seconds to think before choosing your words. Then you will respond by choice and react by decision rather than impulse. Plant words of life and reap rapport and relationship.

In every work that he began in the service of the house of God, in the law and in the commandment, to seek his God, he did it with all his heart. So he prospered.

2 CHRONICLES 31:21 NKJV

Stellar Effort

You can be committed to many things. You may be committed to being successful, achieving goals, building a reputation, serving customers, producing quality products—the list is exhaustive. There is one area in particular that you must be committed to as well. You must be mindful of serving God. Working hard, generating profit, and demonstrating net growth are not enough. Seeking to please God is what it takes to be prosperous. The truth found in 2 Chronicles 31:21 is important because it establishes the precedent for prosperity—an advantage every leader desires to achieve. To become truly prosperous, you must seek God and serve others.

Your efforts must be excellent in serving God's purposes. You can achieve this even if your organization is not a ministry. Carefully honor God personally and professionally by serving others. You are his representative of grace and compassion to those around you.

> **Seeking to please God is what it takes to be prosperous.**

If you seek to please God with all your heart, then you will prosper. You please God when you serve others on his behalf. Your people profit personally when your organization prospers not only monetarily, but spiritually, socially, and educationally. Making a stellar effort can be as simple as writing a note of encouragement, sharing a meaningful Scripture, or lending a helping hand. The bottom line really is prosperity for others.

Identify someone in your organization who has had a difficult week. Decide how you can help him prosper spiritually or socially today. Then serve God by serving him.

You should teach people whom you can trust the things you and many others have heard me say. Then they will be able to teach others.

2 Timothy 2:2 ncv

Multiply Your Effort

You endeavor to surround yourself with people who are emerging leaders. But knowing when leaders in training are ready to lead for themselves can be uncertain. The Bible explains that faithfulness and capability are two qualities that you should look for in future leaders.

As a head coach of a football team, you would place players in positions where they would have the most optimal effect for the team. Let's say there is one player who is faithful to practice. He runs each wind sprint with all he has because of his drive to be the best. He is faithful to the weight room because his desire is to be the center on the offensive line. The problem is that he weighs 138 pounds instead of the needed 280 pounds. He would not be a good fit for that position because he is not able, even though he is faithful. Meanwhile, there is another player who can throw the ball a country mile. He is lean and quick and certainly is able to be the quarterback. But he arrives late to

> **Your job is to help develop the missing quotient through mentoring of the leaders in training.**

practice and doesn't fully participate. He is able, but he is not faithful. Both of these players could develop into vital team members if they were coached to strengthen their weaknesses.

Your job is to help develop the missing quotient through mentoring of the leaders in training. By teaching them to be both faithful and able, you will develop their individual leadership capabilities as well as their collective effectiveness for your team.

~∭◎

Assess those around you with leadership potential. Help them develop their faithfulness or capability to become successful leaders by mentoring them as their leadership coach.

A wicked man hardens his face, but as for the upright, he establishes his way.

PROVERBS 21:29 NKJV

Counterfeit Leaders

A fine line exists between confidence and arrogance. Confident leaders are self-assured enough to believe that they are competent in their abilities. Arrogant leaders are self-deceived enough to believe in their abilities alone. Of course, there are also counterfeit leaders who are just trying to fake it until they make it. Others will decide if they want to follow you based on their confidence in your ability to lead them, so your self-assurance is vital to your leadership.

If you cannot genuinely convince yourself, you will never convince them!

In his "looking glass theory," Charles Cooley explained that a person forms his or her self-perception from three sources: who others think you are, who you think you are, and who you think others think you are. If any of those perceptions are out of balance, you may develop an unrealistic ego, self-doubt, or paranoia. You also must

> **The confident leader is self-assured enough to believe that he is competent in his abilities.**

consider another perspective . . . who God says that you are. In the Scripture, you are called God's beloved, an oak of righteousness and a friend of God.

When you balance God's image of you with others' images of you, together with what you know of your abilities and strengths, you are better able to form a healthy confidence that compels others to follow you. You do not have to fake it until you make it. You can be sure of yourself, even when you aren't sure of the situation.

If you want to have committed followers, you must be a confident leader. To be the real deal, begin to see yourself with the potential that God sees in you.

297

Being afraid of people can get you into trouble, but if you trust the LORD, you will be safe.

PROVERBS 29:25 NCV

Leadership Paralysis

Have you ever felt stuck? You know, stuck, when you find yourself wedged between a rock and a hard place, where you are doomed if you do and doomed if you don't? If you have not yet been stuck, be assured—every leader will arrive at this place of decision paralysis. Immobility sets in because of your need of approval from other people. Your desire to be liked by your peers looms in the back of your mind, stalling your decision or action. This motionless place is where you are unable to carry out your decisions or even make them for fear of what others will think.

No matter how tough a leader you are, you do not want to lose friends or make enemies. You don't want your integrity or ability questioned. However, God has given you an expansive vision for your organization. You have a global perspective beyond what your constituents may understand. When you are stuck, you must remain the strong leader and make the tough decisions in spite of what the human opinion poll may reveal.

> **God specifically promises that if you put your trust in him, he will protect you even when you are stuck.**

Thankfully, God specifically promises that if you put your trust in him, he will protect you even when you are stuck. The wisdom found in this particular proverb is especially important for the leader to remember, for if you seek to please God instead of your employees, customers, or peers in every decision, you can trust that God will protect your reputation and relationships, thereby enabling your effectiveness as a leader.

Leading by fear of others disables your efficacy in decision making, but focusing on faith in God enables your success in leading your organization to effectiveness.

Steep your life in God-reality, God-initiative, God-provisions. Don't worry about missing out. You'll find all your everyday human concerns will be met.

MATTHEW 6:33 MSG

God-Focus

Do you see the glass as half empty or half full? Do you find yourself worrying what you will do if you don't make your budget at the end of the month? Are you often needing more to feel secure? As a leader, you have responsibilities and realities that carry financial burdens. You realize that if you do not make sales happen, then payroll could be affected. You carry the burden of not only feeding your family but all your staff members' families, too. That reality can be worrisome. So, maintaining a God-focus is important to your peace of mind in the realities of leadership.

God-reality is faith. When you look at the glass, see that it is half full, but see the potential for even more. Know that God has provided for you, and believe that he is the source of all your needs. Look at what he has given to you in material resources and human resources with innovation. Think of the lemon. It is just a flavorful fruit. But with a little creativity, it is a resource for lemonade, lemon pie, lemon cake, lemon air freshener, even lemon cleansers.

Maintaining a God-focus is important to your peace of mind in the realities of leadership.

True contentment comes when you focus your mind not only on furthering your own business success, but also on furthering God's initiatives. When you focus on God's methods and trust him to provide what you need for success, you do not have to concentrate on lack. You can be content with the resources that God provides to meet your needs.

God-provisions often come in common packages, but have significant possibilities. Think beyond what is in your hand, and expand your thinking to the reality of God-provision.

Well-spoken words bring satisfaction;
well-done work has its own reward.

PROVERBS 12:14 MSG

A Handy Reward

Growing a business is like farming a garden. A good farmer knows that farming requires more than just planting a few seeds to harvest. First, he must determine what crop he wants to harvest and choose the right season to plant his crop. Next, he must prepare the soil by tilling and nourishing it. Finally, he plants, fertilizes, and waters the seed. The farmer must patiently wait and carefully check the plants' growth and production before anything can be harvested.

Like a farmer, you must determine what result you want to achieve. You must also consider timing as you prepare the people to receive your message by cultivating curiosity and engaging interest. Just as the farmer plants his seed, you plant the goal or vision. You must patiently wait and carefully check the fruitfulness of your efforts as the leader. After a long process, the farmer and leader alike can harvest from all their diligence.

This proverb reminds you that hard work does pay off. You are probably the most diligent employee in your company or volunteer in your organization. Leaders usually are. Sometimes you need to stop and remind yourself that your work should focus on the

Leadership requires the diligent spirit of a farmer.

harvest you want to reap, not simply the work itself. Encourage yourself that the harvest will come when you diligently prepare the field and nurture the crop. Leadership requires the diligent spirit of a farmer. When you are diligent in planting and waiting, you will reap according to the work of your hands.

Review your calendar for this week. Are you spending time both planting and harvesting? If not, schedule time to plant some new ideas for growth, or harvest results by completing an item in your calendar.

H‌e has shown you, O man, what is good; and what does the Lord require of you but to do justly, to love mercy, and to walk humbly with your God?

MICAH 6:8 NKJV

What to Do When You Don't Know What to Do

Everyone is waiting for your decision. You are stumped. You don't have a clue what to do. You have made the pros and cons list, examined your strengths and weaknesses, asked your advisers, and even polled your leadership team, to no avail. You may have even fasted and prayed. Still, you have no clear direction on what decision to make. What do you do?

Sometimes you find yourself in this predicament. When you are trying to make the greater of two good choices, or maybe the better of two bad choices, it is important to remember the guiding principles of justice, mercy, and humility. These principles can become a checklist for your decision. If you are humbly and mercifully making a just decision, you are probably headed in the right direction.

In your position, you have to prioritize funds, attention, and opportunity. You cannot always treat everyone equally in doing this. When you know that you cannot do what seems fair to everyone, remember to do what is just—honest, right, and equitable. Notice the Scripture doesn't simply state that you should be merciful, but that you should love mercy. So, if you

> When you know that you cannot do what seems fair to everyone, remember to do what is just— honest, right, and equitable.

decide to withhold judgment that someone deserves, you should not do so begrudgingly, but willfully. Finally, you should strive to walk humbly with God. For if you act justly, love mercy, and walk humbly, you may not please everyone, but you will meet God's requirement of you.

When you are facing a difficult situation, consult your checklist: Are you impartial in this choice? Is it merciful? Is this choice made from a humble rather than a prideful attitude?

The first speech in a court case is always convincing—until the cross-examination starts!

PROVERBS 18:17 MSG

The Rest of the Story

Some people call it a gut feeling, while others may name it a sixth sense. Whatever its label, discernment is valuable to you, because many occasions for discernment arise in your week. For instance, you may be fully convinced of a marketing strategy presented, until you hear the second proposal. Sometimes when choosing between options, with all things considered and equal, you just have to decide based on your own intuition.

However, discernment is not impulsive decision making. When you are pressed for time in your day, you can make a decision too quickly simply because the opening argument is convincing. Part of the process of discerning the truth is listening to the rest of the story. It is important to hear all sides of a case before making decisions, especially when dealing with relationship issues. Whether you are mediating a dispute or negotiating a compromise, it is beneficial for you to allow both parties to explain their behaviors, desires, and motives.

> **It is important to hear all sides of a case before making decisions.**

Being thorough benefits you in several ways. First, your staff or customer feels valued because you cared enough to listen. Second, you may be able to get to a hidden cause rather than simply the symptoms of a problem. Third, you collect more information to make a confident decision. Others are looking to you for the answer—proper discovery will give you a keener discernment in providing those answers.

Your organization counts on your ability to be both just and wise in "calling the shots." Discernment is one of your most valuable tools in powerful decision making.

In Christ, there is no difference between Jew and Greek, slave and free person, male and female. You are all the same in Christ Jesus. You belong to Christ, so you are Abraham's descendants. You will inherit all of God's blessings because of the promise God made to Abraham.

GALATIANS 3:28–29 NCV

Equal Opportunity Deployment

Embracing diversity is inviting each person to contribute his or her unique intelligence, creativity, and passion for the common goal of creating a multifaceted reservoir of abilities. You have a kaleidoscope of talents and skills among those around you, whether it is a circle of friends, church community, family, or business. When you appreciate the various strengths of individuals, the whole group is strengthened.

To appreciate the strengths of others, you must provide an opportunity for them to utilize their abilities. Develop

trust with a broader range of employees by providing opportunities for them to prove their capabilities. Before you
assign a new project, search your staff
for someone who can develop with the
assignment. Cross training and peer
training are great ways for you to
make learning opportunities available to
less-experienced staff members while
utilizing experts as mentors. Moms are

> **To appreciate
> the strengths of
> others, you must
> provide an
> opportunity for
> them to utilize
> their abilities.**

often great at allowing older siblings to teach younger siblings.
The same concept is effective with adults. The more you teach
others, the more you learn.

Make an intentional effort to broaden diversity. Invite
new friends to your child's next play date. Deploy the young
in the good ol' boy system. Send the woman into the man's
world. Allow the expert to challenge the rookie. Do not let
professional or cultural norms dictate opportunities. A
diverse team stimulates creativity and builds people socially
and professionally.

~))◎

Invite a diverse group of friends for coffee or dinner to discuss a project or just learn about one another. You may be
surprised at the hidden talents of those around you.

By helping each other with your troubles, you truly obey the law of Christ.

GALATIANS 6:2 NCV

Hugs and Handshakes

Technology is great. It offers quick transfer of information, faster production processes, and immediate access to resources. However, reliance on technology has also brought with it dissociation from coworkers and customers. Technology lacks the human factor. For example, many school systems and large corporations now use automated services to receive call-ins from sick staff members. Although the system relieves the need for staff and is more efficient in handling the calls, there is no empathy expressed to the sick staff member.

With the luxury of e-mail, voice mail, and fax machines, workers can go for hours, even days, with no real contact with coworkers, customers, or even their bosses. But people

still have the need for a sense of belonging and purpose that comes through human touch and conversation. So, what are you to do as a leader? Where is the balance? Helping others with their troubles is a prime opportunity not only to please God but also to meet people's needs.

Take advantage of the opportunity to connect with others. The power of a handshake, hug, or pat on the back can bring hope to a discouraged staff member. Although an e-mail note of encouragement is better than no comment at all, it still is not as powerful as a personal conversation. Have a face-to-face encounter when expressing encouragement.

> **Where is the balance? Helping others with their troubles is a prime opportunity not only to please God but also to meet people's needs.**

Show empathy with a personal touch. Congratulate successes. Make eye contact to connect with others. These actions create a sense of belonging and caring in a sometimes cold and isolated world.

Slow down. Notice people's expressions. Does someone seem extraordinarily cheerful? Ask them why. Do you notice someone's hurried and frazzled demeanor? Stop and extend a hand or a hug. You could make another person's day.

$\mathbf{D}$o you not know that those who run in a race all run, but one receives the prize? Run in such a way that you may obtain it.

1 CORINTHIANS 9:24 NKJV

Gold-Medal Leader

Often, the difference between the runner who wins and the runner who loses is the motivation of the runner. Trophies are not enough to motivate the tenacity needed for a 10K marathon. However, more intangible rewards, such as integrity, compassion, and courage, can be the fuel that keeps the runner in the race to win. An inner motivation must fuel the leader to run a winning race.

Without a goal, you have no reason to press toward what lies ahead. You can create goals for every area of your life, including family and spiritual goals. Equally as important as the goal is the real reward of achieving the goal. What you really want to gain from the experience is sometimes more than the superficial tangible prize. If your goal is to have the highest sales and win a cruise, decide what you really want out of that goal. It could be that you do not really want the prestige or honor of being the most productive sales

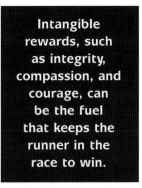

Intangible rewards, such as integrity, compassion, and courage, can be the fuel that keeps the runner in the race to win.

associate, but that you want to spend time with your family vacationing on the cruise. So, the motivating fuel would be your love for your family.

In leadership and in life, the goal is to finish your race. The way that you run your race will determine if your run was worthy of obtaining your prize. Your faithfulness to God and your commitment to others will help you to achieve success in your race. Run your race to win.

Write three goals for this week. For each goal, list the character traits that you will need to move you toward achieving that goal. Target those traits and run your race.

Do to others what you would want them to do to you.

LUKE 6:31 NCV

The Golden Rule

What could be more embarrassing than being told that you have spinach in your teeth? Looking in the mirror at the end of a long day of important meetings and realizing that you had a green-stained smile all day and no one cared enough to tell you is humiliating. How you wish someone had said something. After all, you would have been kind enough to save someone else the same indignity. The golden rule seems simple enough. You have heard it since childhood. But have you ever considered what it is that you want others to "do unto you"? Until you have discovered what you want, you cannot deliver it to others.

Everyone seems to want his or her share of attention, approval, and opportunity from you. The needs of your followers can range from a quick five-minute conversation to guidance on personal issues that affect their professional behaviors. Often, you are aware of needs that even they do not know they have such as training, correction, and motivation. The

> **Have you ever considered what it is that you want others to "do unto you"?**

simplicity of the golden rule provides the essential wisdom you need to fairly divide your attention and approach your delivery.

The wisdom is quite simple. Do for them what you would expect for yourself. This wisdom fits all situations. It can save others embarrassment, provide awareness, or demonstrate concern. If you will treat others the way you want to be treated, you will produce a mutual acceptance and respect that enhances your leadership relationships.

When you doubt whether or not you should address an issue, ask yourself if your comments and behavior toward them are what you would want them to demonstrate toward you.

Remember that I commanded you to be strong and brave. Don't be afraid, because the LORD your God will be with you everywhere you go.

JOSHUA 1:9 NCV

No Man Is an Island

Being Moses's successor in leadership must have been intimidating. Imagine knowing that your mission was to complete the job that even such a great leader as Moses could not accomplish. Joshua was reminded several times to be brave in the tasks ahead of him. Just the foreshadowing of future challenges within this advice would induce apprehension for most. Yet, Joshua did face his mission with courage and strength.

A natural impulse of people in frightening situations is to grab for someone close. Even automobiles have embraced this notion and can provide voice-activated rescue if you become lost or endangered. Somehow just the knowledge that there is someone else sharing in the frightening experience is comforting to those in fear. People seek comfort and courage by clinging to others. Leaders are not very different when

> **Be reminded that you can be bold and courageous because God is with you.**

an intimidating challenge appears. A natural impulse is to call out for someone or something that can bring comfort and dispel your feelings of fear.

If you are new to your position of leadership like Joshua, or if you are a seasoned leader facing a new adventure, your courage can be attacked by fear. In those times, be reminded that you can be bold and courageous because God is with you. You do not have to back down from a challenge or venture because you are intimidated. You do not have to face your fear alone. Grab onto God to capture courage and stand strong.

⁓🙐

If there is a new undertaking that you have been delaying out of intimidation, share the idea with a colleague. When you have another's support, you may gain the confidence you need to conquer your fear.

How much better to get wisdom than gold! And to get understanding is to be chosen rather than silver.

PROVERBS 16:16 NKJV

Money Isn't Everything

Money seems to be the bottom line for so many decisions in business and in families. The quality-versus-quantity debate is discussed between teenagers and their parents and among executive boards of manufacturing companies. At times you must make a decision between the potential of wealth and the opportunity of learning.

Chick-fil-A is an ideal example of this challenge. For sixty years, the company's founder, Truett Cathy, has kept a "never on Sunday" policy in place. The organization firmly believes that their employees should have an opportunity to enjoy family and worship on Sunday if they choose.

Although it has been suggested that the company is jeopardizing profits, Chick-fil-A is satisfied as the nation's second-largest quick-service chicken restaurant chain reporting more than 1.7 billion dollars in 2004 system-wide sales. Another area where Chick-fil-A has been questioned concerning profit possibilities is their franchise opportunities. The company is quite selective in allowing franchises.

> At times you must make a decision between the potential of wealth and the opportunity of learning.

Over the last year, they approved fewer than one hundred applicants out of a pool of more than ten thousand interested buyers. The company is confident that maintaining their standards and values is more important than attaining a higher bottom-line profit.

You may not be in a position to close your business on Sunday, but you may have a choice of whether or not to work on your day of worship. Consider the possibilities, come up with alternatives, weigh your options, and make your decision.

Opportunities to choose wisdom over wealth are all around. Examine your recent choices between earning money and gleaning insight. Be sure you are budgeting your life wisely.

Two people can accomplish more than twice as much as one; they get a better return for their labor. If one person falls, the other can reach out and help. But people who are alone when they fall are in real trouble.

ECCLESIASTES 4:9–10 NLT

I've Fallen, and I Can't Get Up!

God's math doesn't always seem to make sense. If two people work together, you would reason that twice the work could be accomplished. Since this is the Bible, the principle must be universal, and so it seems it is. A team brainstorming new ideas can formulate a more exhaustive and creative list than one person alone. Partners that conquer projects together can finish in a fraction of the time that one could

finish the job. In manufacturing, assembly lines seem to multiply in production exponentially beyond the number of workers on the line.

Everyone has moments of falling. Some people fall behind in their workload. Others fall apart in difficult situations. Having a friend to help you in those times where a free fall is impending is not only comforting, but can also help you maintain your focus on being

> **Friendship is a reciprocal collaboration.**

productive. When you have a friend beside you, he can help keep you from falling in the first place by supporting and encouraging you. Then, if you do begin to slip, he can catch you or help you back onto your feet.

The key to partnership accomplishment seems to be altruism: the willingness of one to reach out and help the other. God said in Proverbs 18:24 that if you want friends, you must show yourself friendly. Friendship is a reciprocal collaboration.

—⫶—

If you have a business partner or spouse, consider how mutual your assistance and encouragement are for each other. Reach out to him or her with a helping hand today.

There is one who scatters, yet increases more; and there is one who withholds more than is right, but it leads to poverty. The generous soul will be made rich, and he who waters will also be watered himself.

PROVERBS 11:24–25 NKJV

Rich Generosity

You give, yet you receive more. You are generous, yet you are made rich. The principle is puzzling. However, look at the number of organizations such as Shriners Hospitals, Ronald McDonald House Charities, and St. Jude's Children's Hospital that give away free services to children in need of serious help. They give generously of their services, but they receive abundantly from others to further fund their giving of more services to others. The principle works: generosity makes you rich.

Many people think of generosity as giving money. But generosity is making what you have to offer available to others, and that can be more than just money. Whatever you have in your hand can be offered. Florida had a record number of hurricanes tear through many counties within only a few weeks' time. Many homes and businesses were without

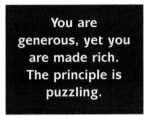

You are generous, yet you are made rich. The principle is puzzling.

electricity, water, even rooftops. The amazing thing about the news reports was that instead of showing people looting those buildings, the majority reported that neighbors were sharing homes, generators, and water. When they compiled all that they had together, they all benefited from each person's contribution.

What you have to offer is of value to someone, whether it is as simple as water or as extravagant as a new car. As you find ways to become more generous, you can expect to be blessed too.

Others need what you have to offer. Whether your wealth lies in your expertise, creativity, or encouragement, extend a gracious offer to help others. Don't wait until someone is in a crisis to be generous.

Search me, O God, and know my heart; test me and know my thoughts.

PSALM 139:23 NLT

God's Stress Test

Cardiologists often use a stress test to reveal the condition of a patient's heart. The exam will indicate if enough oxygen is flowing to the heart. It can also predict whether potential risks of serious problems are present. The procedure of the stress test is for the patient to walk on a treadmill for several minutes. While on his stationary journey, the walker speeds his pace on a progressive incline as the doctor increases the demand for performance. The physically demanding test pushes the heart to a stress point to detect problems and weaknesses.

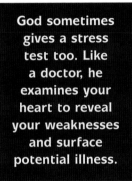
God sometimes gives a stress test too. Like a doctor, he examines your heart to reveal your weaknesses and surface potential illness. Often your heart can be tested by the challenging situations that anger you. When you are pushed to your limit of patience, your words can reveal the condition of your heart. Painful situations can also test your heart's strength. When you are hurt or betrayed, your willingness to forgive is an indicator of a healthy heart.

> **God sometimes gives a stress test too. Like a doctor, he examines your heart to reveal your weaknesses and surface potential illness.**

The purpose of a stress test is to examine the condition of the heart before any damage is done to it. The test reveals what corrections and preventive methods need to be put into place to maintain optimal health. Regular heart checkups, both physical and spiritual, can keep you in a strong condition to fulfill your purpose. So you should guard the condition of your heart.

Ask God to look deep into your heart. If you detect unforgiveness, stress, or anxiety, begin a wellness plan today. Seek ways to decrease your anxiety and increase your peace.

Wise men and women are always learning, always listening for fresh insights.

PROVERBS 18:15 MSG

No Status Quo

Have you ever wondered how household products can seemingly be ever-new and improved? It is as if they are constantly adding new fragrances, uses, and features to products that have been around for years. If the product itself has not changed, then the packaging is at least redesigned frequently. The idea of something being new and fresh is appealing to most people. It intrigues and compels people to try it out, whether it is a product, a theme park ride, or a new menu item at a favorite restaurant.

Wise leaders are always seeking new ideas and innovations. You can find them all around if you are curious enough. Focus groups are often used to test new products, from detergent to toys. But you can use focus groups in many other leadership situations, too. For instance, if you are ready to revamp a policy at work, call together a focus group to discuss a better way of doing it. You can include a variety of stakeholders, from leadership representatives to end users. The collective creative pool may reveal more than you could on your own.

> Many times innovations are born out of complaints or problems.

Often just listening to people's opinions in general conversation can spark new ideas for you. Many times innovations are born out of complaints or problems and the desire to do well. If you are open-minded and willing to probe for insight, you can find new ideas that raise the standard beyond average.

Choose a complaint that you hear often. Think of several creative ways to solve the problem. You will challenge your creative thinking, and you may even find an innovation.

God did not give us a spirit that makes us afraid but a spirit of power and love and self-control.

2 TIMOTHY 1:7 NCV

Power Play

A department manager was upset with a new directive from the company president. He was so upset that he immediately called the president's office and insisted that he speak to the president at once. The secretary explained that she could not connect him at the moment due to the president's ongoing current appointment. The man became even more incensed and asked her if she realized that he was a department manager. She answered that she did know who he was. She then explained that she was only a secretary, but she was the one who connected the calls. He had authority, but she had power.

Authority is vested in a person's position. It is accepted by subordinates because it flows from the top down in the hierarchy of an organization. Many people think that authority is power or influence. But power is simply the ability to get others to do what you want them to do (or not do in the case of the manager's phone call). So anyone can have power regardless of his position.

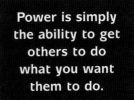

Power is simply the ability to get others to do what you want them to do.

But power can be destructive if it is not balanced with love and self-control. Getting others to do what you want does not have to be done through coercion, punishment, or authority. When power is exhibited through love, your influence on others not only accomplishes your purpose but values others.

Realize your impact on others. Exhibit a loving power that is in the best interest of those you influence. Ensure that the other person gains esteem or success through your actions.

The LORD repay your work, and a full reward be given you by the LORD.

RUTH 2:12 NKJV

Cha-Ching!

The waitress seemed quite frustrated that she was doing most of the work serving the large party seated at the tables shared by her coworker. Her fellow waitperson had a reputation for slacking off on his share of the labor while always demanding his half of the tip. Although the tip for service was quite generous, the waitress did not feel that she was receiving her full reward for all her effort.

Often the hope of financial prosperity drives you to labor hard in the workplace, only to discover that you share the wealth with someone less industrious. A seller's real estate agent often splits his commission with the buyer's agent. Salespeople sometimes share their bonuses with their managers or associates. Business partners may receive equitable dividends regardless

> **True prosperity is the receipt of God's rewards.**

of their individual diligence and commitment to the success. Many professionals will never be paid their worth. After all, how can you put a value on saving lives, educating minds, or restoring families? Yet, firefighters, soldiers, teachers, and social workers do not earn high incomes as compared to other professionals.

If you seek to receive prosperity through only monetary rewards, you may be disappointed. True prosperity is the receipt of God's rewards. Sometimes God's blessings will come in the form of financial gain. However, God also recognizes you with intangible rewards like favor among others, a stellar reputation, a happy family, or good health. Allow God to choose your rewards, and you will have a prosperous life.

⁓🕮

Make a list of all the blessings in your life with which God has rewarded you lately. Especially remember to list the intangible rewards you have received.

Jesus said to those Jews who believed Him, "If you abide in My word, you are My disciples indeed. And you shall know the truth, and the truth shall make you free."

JOHN 8:31–32 NKJV